MW01118472

IMAGES
of America

WHITEWATER

My Dream

If all the knowledge inked in books
    Could be in one great text,
With one great title on its front
    And only one index,
The words that I would like to see
    Upon that mighty cover,
Would be imprinted much like this:
    "To love your fellow-brother."
And then if man from sea to sea
    Would read the script therein,
And understand its mighty facts
    And realize his sin,
Then thoughts would change from
    Those of crime,
Of greed and cruel-aggression,
    To those of universal love
And brotherly affection.
    If in this world of want and war
A union could be met,
    With brotherhood its mighty
    head
And God its legal set,
    Then life would thrive and man
    would live,
And peace would rule supreme,
    and I would know a world,
    which now
To me is but a dream.

            – Paul Ostrander

MY DREAM. Paul Ostrander was the son of Rev. Dr. Clinton Ostrander, pastor of the Congregational Church in Whitewater. The poem was written in 1942, when Paul was 17 years old, and printed in the *Whitewater Register* on November 9, 2000. (*Whitewater Register.*)

On the cover: a scene from one of Whitewater's greatest events, the Home Coming Parade of 1907. The carriages shown are conveying the featured speakers for the festivities up Main Street. (Whitewater Historical Society.)

IMAGES
of America

WHITEWATER

Fred G. Kraege

ARCADIA
PUBLISHING

Copyright © 2006 Fred G. Kraege
ISBN 978-1-5316-2399-9

Published by Arcadia Publishing
Charleston SC, Chicago IL, Portsmouth NH, San Francisco CA

Library of Congress Catalog Card Number: 2005933801

For all general information contact Arcadia Publishing at:
Telephone 843-853-2070
Fax 843-853-0044
E-mail sales@arcadiapublishing.com
For customer service and orders:
Toll-Free 1-888-313-2665

Visit us on the Internet at www.arcadiapublishing.com

CONTENTS

ACKNOWLEDGMENTS

I was inspired to assemble this book to commemorate the 100th anniversary of the *Early Annals of Whitewater*, published in this city in 1906. No history can be compiled without the combined efforts of those who were interested in the past that left their stories behind in print and in pictures. I know I cannot include everyone who has passed along items and pictures for my array of books. To my friends who have passed along treasures that have been saved for future generations, each has a place in this book of the past.

When I began my research in the mid-1980s, the White Memorial Library director, Virginia Follstad, gave me the go-ahead to use the facilities in search of facts about area cemeteries (all 31), in return for the records when they were completed.

I must mention the Whitewater Historical Society and its books, papers, and pictures that I enjoyed gleaning facts from when I was an attendant on the days it was open to the public. Whitewater had a fabulous early history. I thank Doris and Alfred Kolmos for their leadership and for allowing me to browse at random for facts and fodder.

I thank Carol Cartwright of the Historical Society for her patience, determination, and expertise; Marilyn Fuerstenberg for her willingness to help however needed; and Alan Luckett for carefully scanning that which could not be sent to the publishers. I thank Jim Caldwell for encouraging me to contact Arcadia, which has been a fine press to work with. And, once again, thanks to all of the "girls" at the library for bearing with me.

For the use of many of the images in this book, I thank the Whitewater Historical Society and the Irvin L. Young Memorial Library, along with many individuals who have generously lent items from their collections.

Last, but not least, Kristine Zaballos, for making this book a reality, for her offer to serve as production editor, and for helping me to complete these images of Whitewater.

—Fred Kraege

INTRODUCTION

Whitewater is located in the extreme northwest corner of Walworth County, Wisconsin, at the convergence of two streams, an area coveted by Native Americans and later settlers because of the sustenance it provided.

One stream originated in the hills to the southeast, a natural divide of the watershed in this part of the state. The second began six miles to the southwest, where a spring continually bubbled forth its abundance of power for the future.

The Native Americans set up their dwellings along the streams, making use of the clear waters and the abundance of fish that populated these courses. They also hunted wild game throughout the area on trails leading to the surrounding countryside. Earlier natives to Wisconsin apparently cherished this site, as they left a lasting impression on it in the form of effigy mounds to the west of the settlement.

Outsiders disrupted this life and forced most of the native inhabitants from the area in 1832, when about 200 men serving under General Atkinson (including one Abraham Lincoln) pushed them on to the west, across the Mississippi River.

BEFORE THE SETTLERS CAME. The *Early Annals of Whitewater*, published in 1906, described the area that was to become Whitewater as "deserted Indian dwellings along the banks of a stream among oaks left by a former tribe." This is a painting of what Whitewater might have looked like in 1836, when Alvah Foster passed through the area and staked a claim (by carving his name into a tree), but did not return to use it. Apparently a local artist, Helen Wehler, used this as her subject and later presented the painting to the Whitewater Historical Society. (Whitewater Historical Society, hereafter WHS.)

By 1837, settlers seeking land were filtering into the area. They prized not only the fish and the wild game, but above all else the streams for their potential use as water power. At first there was a quiet group of settlers banding together for survival with only the primitive trails leading to wherever the needs of the inhabitants led.

The railroad came in 1852, and a rapid growth of industry followed, ending abruptly in 1892 when the industry that had built the city abruptly abandoned it. Men left their homes in search of jobs when two factories that had employed about 700 laborers closed their doors. The farmers, the storekeepers, and the growing Whitewater Normal School (founded in 1868) can be thanked for keeping the economy at an even keel throughout a lengthy period of flat economic and population growth.

In 1907, an effort was made to instill some spirit in the community with a "Home Coming" event. Business and civil leaders called for former residents to come back for a four-day gala reunion of parades, gatherings, and celebratory events. It was the greatest event that Whitewater has ever known.

The city finally began to grow again after World War II. Like many American cities, some irreplaceable monuments were lost to "progress" before a spirit of preservation—an echo of the Home Coming of 1907—began to prevail. Today, Whitewater maintains a deep appreciation for its agrarian, industrial, and educational roots.

NATIVE AMERICAN MOUNDS. One of the state's best groupings of Native American effigy mounds was included in the 60-acre claim of Samuel Prince, Whitewater's first settler, in 1837. Many years later, the land was used for pasture by farmer Ralph Tratt. This later photograph depicts what the site might have looked like in 1837, and would look like today if it were kept clear of undergrowth. (Author.)

5-28-'96

THE OLD INDIAN TRAIL.

The following poem was written by Mr. S. S. Steele, of this city and won the second prize in the Milwaukee Sentinel's authors' contest reported in last Sunday's paper. As its subject is somewhat akin to the editor's Blackhawk paper in last week's REGISTER we have asked the privilege of giving it to our readers.

This Trail passed very near the present site of Whitewater. The writer knew it well from the Spring on the Stephen Burrows farm west to Lake Koshkonong. It was known as the Old Indian Trail among all the settlers of that section.

A deep worn Trail of Ancient make
Went out from shore of western lake.
An Indian Trail of unknown date,
Relic of tribes cut off by fate.
A thousand years before we came
This Trail was lit by camp-fire flame.
This Trail was red with warrior's blood
Before the Pilgrims crossed the flood.
Here hero brave long years ago
This war path trod to meet h's fo';
Out on these plains along this trail,
The dusky warrior must not fail.
The best his savage heart held dear
His home, his tribe, his all, were here.
The hunter's feet in silence came
This way in chase of wary game
And early caught from hunter's part
The Indian warrior's stealthy art,
No eye more quick, no hand more deft
Where club or knife or arrow cleft,
In chase or war, he stood supreme
In Love, the forest maiden's dream.
Ah, Love! was't here in ancient day
That Cupid learned the hunter's way?
Is this where Cupid found his dart
With aim unerring for the heart?
I'm sure of this, that wild or tame
The heart of man is still the same,
That Lover then in savage days
Presaged our dainty modern ways.
Along this Trail the mother pressed
Her first born savage to her breast.
Knew all the depth in rougher mold
Of love, a mother's heart may hold.
The savage life here swept along
Through unknown ages deep and strong,

O! how those silent Indian feet
Wear deep the Trail and oft repeat
Their tragedy of heathen fears
Through all the centuries of years!
They lived, and loved, they warred and died.
Can nothing but a Trail abide?
This faded Trail perchance began
With ancient pre-historic man.
What countless millions of their race
Have found oblivion's burial place.
How came they here? No man may tell
Oblivion keeps their story well
They were—They're gone. Is this the lot
Of Heathen Tribes, to be forgot?
Some rude primeval relics found
Inside an ancient burial mound,
Some dim traditions light the way
Backward with but feeble ray.
Their generations came and went
Through all the ages, fruitless spent.
A heathen mid night; over all
Unlighted darkness, like a pall.—
One glim'ring ray, alone was found,
Their hope of Happy Hunting Ground.
One single beam, one ray of light
In all that wilderness of night
From Manitou, our God of Love
A single message from above.
Along this Trail they heard his voice
Perhaps—but dim—made him their choice
Too late! Their savage reign is past
Their day of doom arrived at last.
Along this Trail I saw them go
In single file—reluctant—slow,—
The white man's rifle ever pressed
Their ling'ring footsteps toward the west.
I saw their warriors faint and quail,
And fly, along this very Trail.—
The last of all their race went by
Nor uttered one despairing cry,
As silent as their ancient dead
They passed with noiseless Indian tread,
Forever passed, the homes and graves,
Ancestral—long—a line of Braves.
This Trail—their ancient Life's highway
Is covered up and lost to-day
Like those who made it forced to yield
A place for white-man's teeming field,
But looking backward through the years
I still recall the hopes and fears,
That thrilled a pioneering band
Of early settlers in this land,
I sometimes dream, and see the ghost
Of all that countless savage host
Go by again with silent tread
The spirit warriors of their dead.

THE OLD INDIAN TRAIL. This poem appeared in the *Whitewater Register* on May 28, 1896. Spencer S. Steele helped author the book *Early Annals of Whitewater*. (*Whitewater Register*.)

9

One

EARLY WHITEWATER

THE GRIST MILL. They came, they saw, they conquered. Miles from civilization the early settlers built their homes and set up their shops, withstanding the trials of most early settlements. They were an industrious group, coming from the northeast and following what had been taught them in their "home communities," making use of water power, hunting and fishing, and raising crops. The settlers united with others to set up homes in the surrounding countryside and the fledgling village, creating a bond that knew no end. Merchant, miller, cobbler, doctor, lawyer, laborer, and homemaker; all worked in unison to build one community. The fathers and mothers were creative, innovative, and ambitious. What a story they left, if only all might know it. They made the most of life without its modern conveniences. In 1839, the smaller wooden portion of the Old Stone Mill, shown at the right of the photograph, was built. This 1870s photograph is one of the earliest known of the mill. (WHS.)

WHITEWATER'S FIRST HISTORIAN. Prosper Cravath was, for many years, the foremost citizen of Whitewater. In 1840, he surveyed and platted the village for James Trippe, the original proprietor of the town site. Using Trippe's Mill as the town center, he laid streets that radiated from it like the spokes of a wheel. Cravath practiced law, was a member of the first state legislature in 1848, held various local offices, and was Whitewater's postmaster from 1872 to 1880. He wrote historical sketches of Whitewater in 1858 that were published in the *Whitewater Register*, sketches which, after the beginning of the 1900s, became part of the book *Early Annals of Whitewater*. In the "Introductory" to that book, he wrote, "In offering for publication . . . this accounting of the settlement of our village . . . I have been led to make these communications that those who come among us at a later date may know what has been done by these noblemen who first pitched their tents in this then wilderness . . . and may know them for what they were, a band of energetic, noble, strong-hearted men and women, ever ready to go to work for public as well as private good." (WHS.)

LETTER OF SOLOMON JUNEAU. Solomon Juneau died in the fall of 1856. Many of our early arrivals knew him through their trade in Milwaukee. A great burial display honoring him was attended by both settlers and Native Americans from the surrounding sites they still called home. A statue in his honor was unveiled in Milwaukee in 1887. This letter to the editor was printed in the *Whitewater Gazette*, July 3, 1856. (*Whitewater Gazette*.)

THE ORIGINAL.—The following letter from Hon. Solomon Juneau, one of the oldest and best known pioneers of the State, gives us another name for Whitewater. Mr. J. has our most sincere thanks for the valuable information.

Our readers will remember that a few weeks ago we published a communication from Ex-Governor Doty, giving "Waubish Nepaywau," as the Menomonee name of our river—signifying the white water.

THERESA, June 26th, 1856.

Editor of the Whitewater Gazette:

VERY DEAR SIR :—Your letter of May 26th, was by accident mislaid, and found it to-day. The river Whitewater is called by the united tribes of Chippewa, Ottaway, and Pottawathmies, *Wau-be-gan-nau-po-kat,* meaning, rily, whitish water, caused by white, soft clay, in some parts of it.

Any information in regard to Indian names will be cheerfully given by me, at any time, when requested.   Yours, very truly,

SOLOMON JUNEAU.

A Merry Briton in Pioneer Wisconsin

A contemporary narrative reprinted from

LIFE IN THE WEST:
*Back-Wood Leaves and Prairie Flowers:
Rough Sketches on the Borders of the Picturesque,
the Sublime, and Ridiculous. Extracts from
the Note Book of Morleigh in Search of an Estate*

published in London in the year 1842.

1950

THE STATE HISTORICAL SOCIETY OF WISCONSIN

Whitewater is decidedly the prettiest little village I have yet seen in this wild country; the villas are built apart, as they ought to be, with great regularity, each having a goodly garden of rich soil; so that, in the words of Goldsmith, "Every rood of ground (may have) maintained its man," even in a town, without the aid of the noble army of capitalists and speculators and their martyrs. There are several Germans, and some very intelligent New-English folks at Whitewater. They have a mill which does not require great water-power; and if the great manufacturer can be kept at bay, they will grow up a happy community, in the midst of a fine agricultural and pastoral country.

A MERRY BRITON IN PIONEER WISCONSIN. This account of Whitewater was published in London in 1842 as part of a narrative entitled *Life in the West: Back-Wood Leaves and Prairie Flowers: Rough Sketches on the Borders of the Picturesque, the Sublime, and Ridiculous. Extracts from the Note Book of Morleigh in Search of an Estate.* It was reprinted in 1950 by the State Historical Society of Wisconsin. A copy may be found in the Irvin L. Young Memorial Library in Whitewater. (*Whitewater Gazette*.)

SAMUEL PRINCE
1791 - 1867
First Settler in Whitewater, July 1837

THE FIRST SETTLER. Samuel Prince staked his claim of 60 acres in the spring of 1837. It included a group of Native American mounds on the western edge of the city, now a city park. Alone, he set up a crude 12-foot-by-12-foot log cabin. A number of the early settlers spent time with him in this "castle" as they prepared their new homes. (WHS.)

A TOWN MATRIARCH. Rosepha Ann Comstock Trippe was the wife of Dr. James Trippe, who built Whitewater's first gristmill and sawmill. He became the proprietor of the village site, turning over vast areas for its churches, building sites, and cemetery. He died in 1844 and was one of the first to be buried in the new cemetery, on the east side of town. Rosepha Trippe was a leader; she was business-minded and determined to carry on with her husband's work. She died in 1881. (Irvin L. Young Memorial Library, hereafter Library.)

LAYING OUT THE STREETS. David Powers came to Whitewater in 1839 and helped establish the gristmill. He worked for Prosper Cravath, surveying and platting the radiating streets. He became the city's first postmaster and built its first hotel. He and his brothers, Joseph and Samuel, were instrumental in starting up the neighboring communities of Hebron and Palmyra as well. (WHS.)

THE TERRITORIAL OAK. This is one of the trees used as a marker for surveying in the early days when the Territorial Road was staked out from Rochester to Madison, along with the streets in the downtown. The tree and its memorial plaque are located at the corner of Franklin and Main Streets. The house on the corner was the home of Rosepha Trippe. (Library.)

HENRY E. RILE
1840~1922

A PICTORIAL RECORD. Henry E. Rile came to Whitewater as a teenager in 1856. He worked in several of the new brick "blocks," or buildings, downtown, and is best known for his sketches of the buildings in the area. He returned to New York in 1862 and sent many letters to the editor of the *Whitewater Register,* which were published in a number of issues. A collection of these letters can be found in the Irvin L. Young Memorial Library in Whitewater, for good reading. (WHS.)

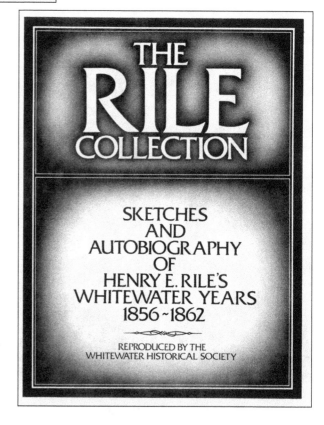

THE RILE COLLECTION

SKETCHES AND AUTOBIOGRAPHY OF HENRY E. RILE'S WHITEWATER YEARS 1856~1862

REPRODUCED BY THE WHITEWATER HISTORICAL SOCIETY

THE RILE COLLECTION. In 1857, townspeople were worried to see a stranger standing in the streets of Whitewater drawing up what was to become a map. It is possible Henry Rile formed a friendship with this man, W. W. Card, and therein found an attraction for sketching pictures and history. Rile's sketches found their way into the *Rile Collection,* published by the Whitewater Historical Society in 1987 to mark the city's 150th anniversary. (WHS.)

MAIN STREET, LOOKING EAST. This Rile sketch shows Trippe's Mill and the bridge across the creek. The milepost for the Territorial Road would have sat in the middle of the stream. This was one of the first roads laid in town; according to the *Early Annals of Whitewater*, the "thirtieth mile post [is] in Whitewater Creek, creek two and a half feet deep." (WHS.)

MAIN STREET, LOOKING WEST. Looking west, the Montour House hovers over the old mill in this sketch. The rooftops of stores lining the north side of the street can be seen, and in the distance, the first brick building to be built on the north side of Main Street, in 1857, alongside of the old Exchange Hotel. The mill pond (now Cravath Lake), on the south side of the street, was formed when a dam was built to provide water power for grinding grain. (WHS.)

MAIN STREET. WHITEWATER, WISCONSIN:

THE SOUTH SIDE OF MAIN STREET, 1861. The first brick building with two storefronts was called the Emporium, built in 1853. The next store, the Commonwealth Block, also with two storefronts, was erected in 1855 by G. H. Smith and C. E. Curtice. B. O. Bailey started the next single store in 1853; then came the large Central Block, built by William Birge, James Worm, and O. P. Congor in 1856; and the last three-story building was erected by Sanger Marsh in 1855. Despite 150 years of fires and renovations, the city's skyline is very similar today. A telltale feature long gone is the Republican Pole, also called the Liberty Pole, that stands in the center of this drawing. It was erected in 1860, when Abraham Lincoln was in the race for the presidency. A Democratic Pole was erected on the other end of First Street and is seen over the second set of stores. Both were over 100 feet in height. The Democratic Pole succumbed to the elements first, and the Republican Pole was destroyed by lightning at 6:00 a.m. in the middle of May in 1889. On the right side are the stores consumed by fire in 1867 and gradually rebuilt into the buildings seen today. (WHS.)

THE NORTH SIDE OF MAIN STREET. This entire block, including the Montour House and the frame stores on the north side of the street, burned down in 1867. Early merchants were Bassett, Beckwith, Stanton, LeBaron, Peck, Brady, Patterson, Pratt, Babcock, Earle, Sanford, Wakely, and Starin. (WHS.)

THE NORTH SIDE OF MAIN STREET, SECOND BLOCK, 1860. The Exchange Hotel was dedicated on July 4, 1842, in the city's first elaborate celebration. The brick building, the first to be built on the north side of the street, was erected in 1857. The saddle shop of Joe Haubert, a marble shop of Simon D. Wright, a meat market of Dobell and Lawrence, Victor Egloff's Jewelry store, and the grocery store of R. N. Ensign stand up the street. (WHS.)

NORTH SIDE OF MAIN STREET. This was the first brick building on the north side of Main Street in block two. It was built by Charles E. Curtice, who had purchased the Exchange Hotel, on the right, renaming it the Commercial House. The store next door to the west was the grocery/dry goods store of A. Wahlstedt (pictured), and the next one the harness shop of Joseph Haubert, who could boast of having the first plate-glass window in town. (WHS.)

THE NORTH SIDE OF MAIN STREET, PRIOR TO 1900. This photograph, taken near First Street in the late 1890s, shows the Exchange Hotel and the livery sign. The hotel became known as the Kinney House for a number of years before being razed at the beginning of the 20th century. (WHS.)

THE OLD RED MILL. The Red Mill was built by Asaph Pratt in 1843 on the site that the golf course occupies today, just south of the city. It served as a gristmill, distillery, cheese factory, and various other industries. It was fitted to generate electricity, but lost so much power over the transmission lines that it was abandoned. The dam was dynamited in 1902, ending its productive life. The resulting marshland was returned to farmers upstream. (WHS; Scholl Collection.)

THE OLD STONE MILL. This photograph shows the mill in the second decade of the 20th century, about 69 years after it was built. In June of 1871, a water wheel and force pump for Engine House No. 1 of the newly-formed fire department were placed in position. Several hundred feet of water main, with force enough to shoot a stream of water over 100 feet into the air, were laid in the business district. The tower above and beyond the mill was used to hoist the fire hose to dry it out. (Library.)

THE PAPER MILL. The newly-erected paper mill, in this sketch by Rile, was located on the site of the old sawmill, which was built by James Trippe in 1841. It burned a few years before this mill was erected in 1859. The dam had been washed away in 1856 and it, too, had to be set up for the new mill. (WHS.)

PAPER MILL PHOTOGRAPH BY WILLIAM MITCHELL. This photograph of the paper mill was taken in either 1865 or 1866 by William Mitchell, a local photographer. The paper mill, which made a variety of paper, had several owners in the course of its 30-year history. The building stood idle for nearly 20 years until 1913, when the Libby-McNeil and Libby Condensery began operations there. An article in the *Whitewater Register* in 1921 stated this mill was the first paper mill in Wisconsin. (WHS.)

Two

EXPLOSIVE GROWTH

BUSY, BUSY, BUSY! After Whitewater's settlers established a downtown and small businesses to meet the needs of the village, a tremendous boost was given in 1852 when the Milwaukee and Mississippi Railroad chose Whitewater as a stop on its way from Milwaukee to Prairie du Chien. The original plan was to dig a canal from the Milwaukee area to the Rock River, but with the railroad making progress in the East, the railroad won out. Local merchandise found an outside market, most notably the plow and wagon manufactory of Winchester, DeWolf and Partridge and the Esterly reaper works on the east side. These two manufacturers had top-selling products that made Whitewater a bustling industrial town. The businesses had their ups and downs; occasional fires led to the destruction of some of their buildings. Yet, these manufacturers were indebted to those who labored for them and rebuilt. The explosive industrial growth led to village incorporation in 1858. This photograph shows a terrific view of the south side of Main Street, just prior to 1881. Until 1842, this block was intended to be the commons, as found in villages and cities in the eastern part of the country. (Library; Fran Achen Collection.)

THE FIRST RAILROAD. As railroads became the rage in the East, Wisconsin jumped on the bandwagon. An engine was brought to Milwaukee on a schooner and served on the first rail line in the state. The rails reached Whitewater in 1852, with regular service beginning in January of 1853. It was known as the Milwaukee and Mississippi Railroad and later became part of the Chicago, Milwaukee, and St. Paul Railroad (the Milwaukee Road). (Whitewater Register.)

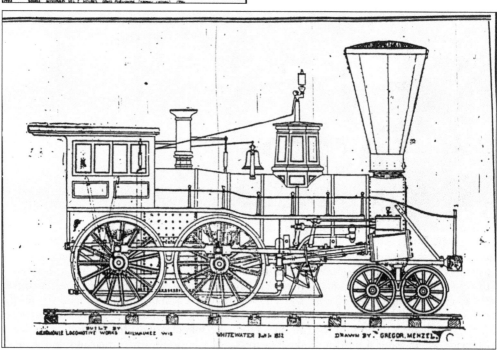

OLD ENGINE WHITEWATER. An article in the local paper in 1902 called this the "first engine built in Wisconsin"—actually, it was the second. These first "iron horses" were named after the new stations established along the rail lines. On its trial run, the first engine covered 14 miles in 12 minutes, over 60 miles an hour, to great acclaim. The engine was destroyed in a collision east of Palmyra, Wisconsin, a few years later. (Milton Couriero.)

THE WHITEWATER HOTEL. The original hotel on this site on Whitewater Street was erected shortly after the railroad came to the community in 1852. Built by Luther Cadmun, it was called the Cadmun House, American House, and later, the Whitewater Hotel. It burned in May 1892, but was quickly rebuilt and today looks much the same as it does in this *c.* 1900 photograph. (WHS.)

THE COURTLAND HOUSE. The Badger State House was built in 1853–1954 by Morris Ensign, directly across the street from the railroad depot. In 1863, Giles Kinney bought and remodeled it and changed its name to the Cortland House, in the course of time also known as the Courtland House. There was a succession of owners until the building was demolished in 1966 for the building of the new city hall and police and fire department building. (WHS.)

WINCHESTER & PARTRIDGE MANUFACTURING COMPANY. Lucius Winchester arrived in Whitewater in 1844 and went into the blacksmith business. In 1853, William DeWolf joined Winchester and combined the blacksmith with his plow factory. In 1855, they constructed a large factory on Whitewater Street, down from the Old Stone Mill, making a variety of plows for the different soils and employing about 30 men. John S. Partridge joined, opening a store and advertising their products to the market. In competitions and fairs their products ranked highly. In 1865, wagon production began in earnest and became the main part of their production. DeWolf left the ranks, and the firm became the Winchester & Partridge Manufacturing Company. In 1870 about 3,500 wagons and an equal number of plows were

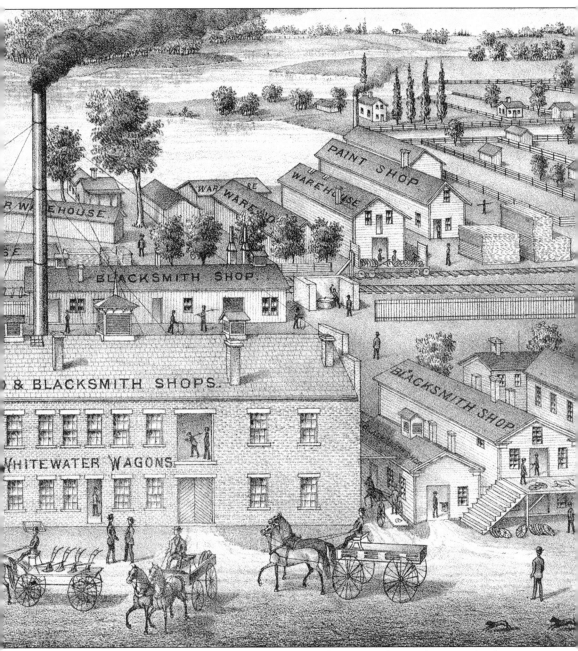

made. The company sold its wagons throughout the United States and Canada. In 1873, when the United States and Canada were planning to lay out the boundary from North Dakota to the Pacific Ocean, Queen Victoria ordered 51 wagons from the company to be used by her Britannic Majesty's North American Boundary Commission. These wagons were chosen for their superior workmanship and reputation, for which the commission paid a premium. For someone who is curious, Montgomery & Ward sold Whitewater Wagons as late as 1931. Could these have been manufactured from the old Whitewater patents? (Zaballos family.)

L. A. WINCHESTER

PURVEYOR OF PLOWS. Lucius A. Winchester arrived in Whitewater in 1844 and established a blacksmith shop that became famous for its plows and wagons (Winchester & Partridge Manufacturing Company) in later years. He worked with several partners in his trade. It was largely because of this company and the Esterly Reaper Works that the village was able to reach city status in 1885. He died in 1890, shortly after closing the factory and selling in 1889. (WHS.)

RESIDENCE OF L. A. WINCHESTER.

THE WINCHESTER HOUSE. The Winchester house was built by Nelson Salisbury on the corner of Esterly Avenue and Main Street in 1867. The house was later owned by Bentley Dadmun, the owner of Dadmun's Feed Mill. This Italianate home has a widow's walk on its roof. The Whitewater Wagon Company's foundry made ornamental castings, and may have made those on both the Winchester and Partridge houses. They made some door casings or frames for downtown stores as well. (Zaballos family.)

A MAN OF ALL TRADES. John S. Partridge was engaged in many of the city's early industries, being in the mercantile business, when the railroad arrived he helped erect "the Big Warehouse" for grain and produce. In 1857, he closed out these operations and joined Winchester in his factory. He held many positions of trust in the city and departed this life in 1892. (WHS.)

THE PARTRIDGE HOUSE. The Partridge home, built in 1856, is on the extreme west end of Center Street. It is a large yellow brick house topped by two widow's walks. A large addition, including the second widow's walk, was made after John Partridge purchased it. There are two white marble and two black slate fireplaces inside the house. (WHS.)

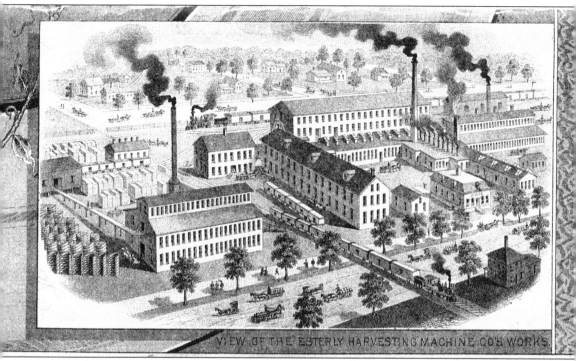

VIEW OF THE ESTERLY HARVESTING MACHINE CO'S WORKS.

Esterly Harvesting Machine Company. George Esterly was one of the first settlers in the area in 1837, locating seven miles southeast of Whitewater in an area known as Heart Prairie. As he owned a huge tract of land and raised wheat, he endeavored to find a better way to harvest it. He looked at several primitive machines around the Midwest and brought back parts; in 1844 he received a patent for his first harvester. He improved on it and entered into competition in Chicago, besting Cyrus McCormick for the first gold medal ever awarded, in 1848. He purchased five acres on the east side in 1856; by the next year, harvesters were being produced and improved, and they continued to be successful in all competitions. More men were employed, and houses were built on the east side, in an area that eventually became known as Reaperville. In addition to reapers, the company made a variety of implements, such as a combined reaper and mower, a seeder, plows, furniture, sleighs, and coffins. Esterly led a failed attempt to bring more industry to the city, in case one or the other large industries should leave. In the peak years, the company employed over 525 men. With the offer of a larger facility nearer the wheat fields, the company moved to the vicinity of Minneapolis in late 1892. (Author.)

ESTERLY'S PATENTED HARVESTING MACHINE. Esterly's reaper was unveiled in an 1845 issue of the *Cultivator*. While not popular, it introduced two ideas used later in harvesting machines. One was the push principle of locomotion. The other is that it may have been the first "header," a form of reaper that captured only the heads of the stalk and left the straw in the field. (Author.)

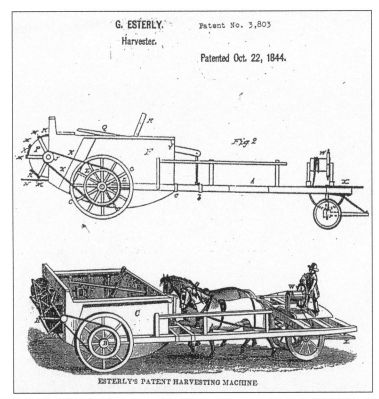

A GOLD MEDAL. This medal was awarded to George Esterly for his first entry at the Second Annual Fair of the Chicago Mechanics Institute, held in 1848. He won again in 1849. In 2003, a number of Esterly descendents reunited in Whitewater, and the medal was on view for all who attended the dinner. The medal remains in the possession of the Esterly family. (Author.)

A HANDSOME PICTURE. From the *Whitewater Register*, March 30, 1872: "Our office has been ornamented the past week with a superb, large size, colored lithograph, left with us by George Esterly, Esq. It is a spirited and beautifully designed picture representing a harvest field in the foreground with two of the Esterly reapers at work; a little beyond in another field one of the seeders is seen sowing newly prepared ground for the next year's crop. In the distance is a beautiful mountain and lake scene. Upon the latter two handsome little boats are sailing, and upon one of the banks, is a sheltered and romantic nook, close by a rocky bluff, the tent of the 'Canvass Back Club' is to be seen with the stars and stripes floating above its patriotic roof. Two of the redoubtable Nimrods are just setting out on a predatory excursion, while a third, down on the shore of the lake is making the feathers fly from a flock of presumptuous mallards, who had dared to remain in such a dangerous vicinity too long for their own good." And, some years later, another account in the *Register* queried, "And just how popular were his reapers? 'Esterly' is the name of a new village and post office on a newly opened railroad in Dakota Territory. The name is given in honor of the Esterly Harvester and Binder, which is very popular in that section and looked upon by the farmers as their best friend." (*Whitewater Register*, August 8, 1884.) The settlement of Esterly was located within Fuller Township, South Dakota. (WHS.)

GEORGE ESTERLY. In describing George Esterly's years in and around Whitewater, one sentence sums it up: "George Esterly was the patriarch of them all." A book called the *LaGrange Pioneers* talks about his influence on that settlement, located seven miles to the southeast of Whitewater. Setbacks and successes were common among early inventors, and Esterly was no exception. But his was the largest industry in Walworth County in the mid-1880s. (WHS.)

THE ESTERLY HOUSE. Esterly purchased the Center Street home of Eleazer Wakely in 1864, at the time described as the finest location in the village. After his death, the premises were sold to the city and transformed into a grade school, which in 1927 was razed for a new high school building, which was in turn taken down in the 1990s. (Library; Fran Achen Collection.)

THANKSGIVING DAY AT THE ESTERLY FACTORY, 1873. A great Thanksgiving Day dinner was held in the new paint and finishing shop to mark its dedication in 1873, shown on this stereo card published by Mr. and Mrs. P. Ersly, local photographers. Esterly invited everyone who had worked or was working in his factory to have dinner together. Other village dignitaries were also present, such as Lucius Winchester, John Partridge, and Prosper Cravath, who spoke to the group of 500 to 600 people. (WHS.)

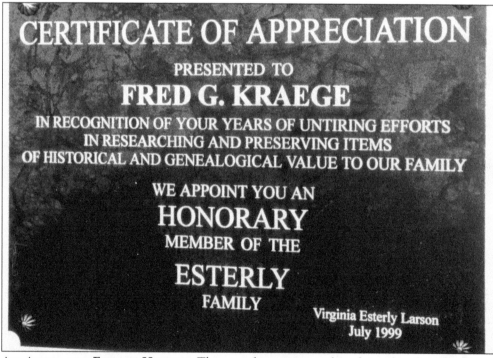

CERTIFICATE OF APPRECIATION

PRESENTED TO

FRED G. KRAEGE

IN RECOGNITION OF YOUR YEARS OF UNTIRING EFFORTS
IN RESEARCHING AND PRESERVING ITEMS
OF HISTORICAL AND GENEALOGICAL VALUE TO OUR FAMILY

WE APPOINT YOU AN

HONORARY

MEMBER OF THE

ESTERLY

FAMILY

Virginia Esterly Larson
July 1999

AN AWARD FOR ESTERLY HISTORY. This award was presented to the author for compiling a history of the Esterly Reaper Works of Whitewater, the most complete history of the company to be found anywhere, which can be viewed at the Irvin L. Young Memorial Library. (Author.)

AN ESTERLY REUNION. Members of the far-flung Esterly family came back to Whitewater for a reunion in September 2003. From left to right are (first row) Fred Kraege, author; (second row) Oscar J. Sorlie, Minnesota; Virginia Esterly Larson, Texas; Thomas Esterly, Maryland; Katie Coe Coleman, Wisconsin; Alan Esterly, Louisiana; Mary Ann Nevel, Wisconsin; Bill Esterly, Mississippi; and Arthur Herman, Wisconsin. (Author.)

OUR "ALBERT EINSTEIN." One of the most noted professors at the Whitewater Normal School was Warren S. Johnson, who worked in the Department of Natural Sciences. He was later dubbed the "Albert Einstein" of the normal school. He invented the thermostat for regulating heat in a room and founded a company, Johnson Controls, which has become one of Wisconsin's most important industries. He also formed the nation's first fleet of postal trucks, in Milwaukee, around 1905. (University of Wisconsin-Whitewater Archives.)

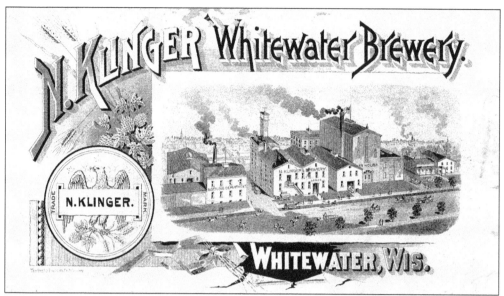

KLINGER'S BREWERY. This is an advertising card for Klinger's Brewery, which began operation in 1859 when George Streng set up shop on the corner of North and Jefferson Streets. William Marshall took over in 1862, having previously been a brewer in Cold Spring. Klinger bought it in 1864 and made beer until 1905. (Author.)

WHITEWATER BREWERY WAGON. In 1907, a new firm began operating in the old Klinger Brewery, the Whitewater Brewing Company. William Fink and William Klann were the brewers who bottled Cream Top, known as the "Beer that Made Milwaukee Furious," until prohibition in 1919. After prohibition, in 1933, the brewery reopened and operated under several owners. Beer was produced in both bottles and cans until closed in 1942. (Library; the brewery.)

KLINGER'S BREWERY AND BREWERY HILL. This stereo card depicts Klinger's Brewery and "Brewery Hill" on North Street. Klinger continued to make improvements in the factory and its brew. It was a major industry in its day. (WHS.)

AN ELEPHANT ON CENTER STREET. This walking brewery advertisement passed in front of where the post office sits on Center Street today. There were plenty of merchants back then to offer great displays to those watching on the sidelines. This card dates from the mid-1890s, note the wooden sidewalks. (Author.)

THE WHITEWATER NORMAL SCHOOL. The Whitewater Normal School was constructed in 1868, with Newton M. Littlejohn and Judge Samuel Austin White heading the building committee. As it was the second state normal school established in Wisconsin, Whitewater competed with many other sites for the privilege. It later became a state teacher's college, a Wisconsin state college, and eventually part of the Wisconsin State University System. In 1972, this system merged with the University of Wisconsin System, and the Whitewater campus became the University of Wisconsin-Whitewater. (WHS.)

GRADUATION DAY, 1877. The inscription on this photograph reads, "For Miss Virginia Deichman, from her grandfather, Dr. John Deichman, of Whitewater, Walworth County, Wis., June 17th 1877." Dr. Deichman had a drugstore downtown and was thought of as a bit of an eccentric for his collection of many unusual things such as stuffed birds, small animals, and reptiles; a cabinet of 500 mineral specimens; shells; and Native American artifacts, all of which were crowded into the shop. (WHS.)

Three

THE SLOWDOWN

THE FLOOD OF 1881. Heavy snows in the early months of 1881 led to flooding in the spring, one of the many natural disasters that plagued the Whitewater area in the 1880s. By April, the high water caused many bridges to be swept downstream. Events such as this were not all that tragic in and of themselves. In addition to the big snows, the village endured fires that leveled several blocks of downtown, crop failures, and recessions. It all took its toll, but the community fought back and overcame its misfortunes. The fires taught them a lesson; they needed protection. After the floods, they built better dams and bridges, improving their mills in the process. The hardest blow was the loss of the cities two large industries, which left the working class with little income. Some businessmen had tried to encourage more industry to locate in the village, but it went for naught. "If you do not heed the advice, and one or both of us (the two large manufacturers) should leave your city, you would become nearly helpless," said George Esterly in a prophesy that was proven correct. Still, the city held on. (WHS.)

THE LONG STAIRWAY. This early 1870s photograph shows the long stairway that led to the *Whitewater Register*'s offices on the second floor of this building on the south side of Main Street. Below is an article written by Edwin D. Coe, editor of the *Whitewater Register*, which appeared in the newspaper on June 7, 1883. (WHS.)

June 7, 1883 WW Reg

When Whitewater was first discovered, full forty-five years ago, two conspicuous objects loomed up in the midst of its verdurous beauty ; one was the tall form of our venerable fellow citizen, Prosper Cravath Esq., the other was a flight of wooden steps, standing firm, erect and solitary in the strange surroundings of forest, river and lake. How that isolated staircase came there, and when and why, were mysteries that knew no fathoming. The traditions of the red men, running back until lost in the mists and haze of the Cimmerian abyss revealed nothing of its beginning. When the village site was platted, and the surveyors radiated out from the well authenticated barrel of "black-strap" on the bridge by the mill, they located the junction of the two main streets of the village just east of the ancient stairway. Then came Joe Bower and began piling up brick buildings all around the town. The advantages offered by the old stairs did not long escape his eagle eye, and in a twinkling he had a brick block built snugly against them. That was long years ago, and fires and the elements did their work, yet the old stairs defied them all, and "Ajax" with the rest. But when, years ago, the old REGISTER office went up in smoke and down in ashes, the new one was established in its present quarters, and the crowds which throng its counting rooms have had to pass up and down the old historic stairway. Under this new stress it finally began to show signs of weakness. Wide cracks appeared : the ends of the steps decayed and parted company with the side supports ; although braced with timbers underneath the strangers climbing up their dizzy heights did not understand their deceptive solidity, and would often come charging into our office with blanched faces and bulging eyes, as though they had escaped the greatest peril of their lives. It was vain to argue with them—they believed the evidence of their own vision and insisted that the stairs only hung to the wall by their eye brows, as it were. Hence, as the people were stubbornly unbelieving and unesthetic, the order was issued to demolish the ancient structure and establish a new one in its place. Those energetic builders, Cutler & Waite, took the case in hand and the final transformation scene was speedily enacted. So, while we still insist that the old stairway was as strong as the new one, we have been willing to recognize the power of the imagination and to admit that it is about as bad to be scared to death as to be killed, and shall be fully rewarded in knowing that the fair ones and the timid can come and see us more comfortably than before.

40

THE SOUTH SIDE OF MAIN STREET, LOOKING WEST. This photograph by John P. Whipple, taken in the 1870s, is of the first block of Main Street. The first double store was called the Emporium. A second set, the Commonwealth, was three stories high, but after a fire it was lowered to two. A single store follows, then the largest on the block, with three stores in it. The skyline today is similar, but a few façades are gone. (WHS.)

AN EARLY PHOTOGRAPH OF MAIN STREET. The building on the right was built by David Powers in the early 1840s and served as a drugstore. In this photograph is John T. Smith's jewelry store. The small building to the left of it is Pierce's gun shop. The tall brick building was erected by S. Clark in 1863. The store to the left of that was Dr. Deichman's drugstore. On the far corner, in the middle of the photograph, is Dr. Warne's drugstore. (Hackett family.)

FOSE MEAT MARKET. This rooftop view was taken in the mid-1870s from the south side of Center Street and Second Street looking northwest. It shows the Fose Meat Market, which opened in October 1873. The building across the street is a part of the old Joseph Pratt wagon shop. The U.S. Express Office is partially shown on the right. Where you see Pratt's shop, you will find the First Citizen's State Bank's parking lot today. (WHS.)

A ROOFTOP VIEW, LOOKING NORTHWEST. This view looks over the tops of stores and horse barns from the south side of Center Street. The Congregational Church stands on the left, and the Whitewater Normal School is in the distance. (WHS.)

THE GREAT SNOW OF 1881. A series of storms hit Whitewater in 1881. One at the end of February lasted 40 hours, blocking roads and the railroad, and another, in early March, closed down the city. The snow was four feet deep. This view shows the north side of Main Street looking south, near the middle of the first block. (WHS.)

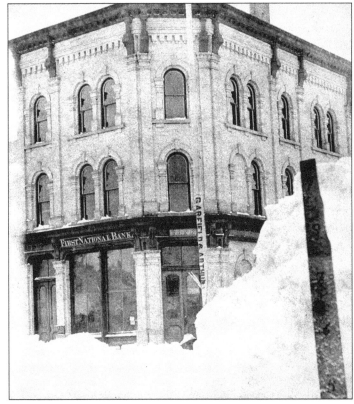

THE CHAMBERLAIN BLOCK UNDER COVER OF SNOW. The First National Bank, on the corner of First and Main Streets, opened its doors in 1863 and later merged with the First Citizen's State Bank. Notice the Republican (Liberty) Pole with its 1880 presidential candidates, James Abram Garfield and Chester Allen Arthur, on it. Put up in 1860, the pole stood in this spot until one morning at 6:00 in the middle May in 1889, when lightening struck and shattered it. (WHS.)

NOTHING BUT SNOW. This is Center Street looking east from a spot near Second Street. There is not much to see but snow. (WHS.)

SNOW ON WHITEWATER STREET. This photograph was taken on Whitewater Street, looking north, with the Whitewater Hotel on the corner (Messersmith, proprietor). In the distance is the rooftop of the Winchester & Partridge Manufacturing Company. (WHS.)

THE SNOW ON FIRST STREET.
This is First Street looking north
toward Main Street. You see
both party liberty poles in this
photograph; the Republican
Pole in the background, on the
corner of Main Street, and the
Democratic Pole in the foreground,
on the corner of Center Street.
Over 100 feet tall, these poles were
maintained and repaired for almost
30 years. (WHS.)

**THE SNOW ON MAIN
STREET.** Glancing over
the snow banks you see
the Bower House, built
in 1879–1880, looming
high with the S. Clark
Building (1863) next
to it. Dr. Deichman's
drugstore, apothecary,
and self-made museum
is the small frame
building. The smallest
building is a harness
manufactory. The top
of a dry goods store and
grocery stands next to
the drug store of Dr.
H. Warne, later owned
by H. J. O'Connor,
which was replaced by
the Commercial Bank
building in 1913. (WHS.)

A FINE PIECE OF WORK. The Union Carriage Works of E. I. Morey made and gave the city its first piece of rolling equipment, like this hook and ladder truck, in 1886. Twenty feet long, it was pulled by men until first horses and later trucks became the source of locomotion. The city agreed to form a volunteer hook and ladder brigade and to find a permanent storage place for the new equipment. (Author.)

THE STATE HOSE CHAMPS OF 1898. The Whitewater Volunteer Fire Department has always had a reputation of being one of the best in the state. The 1898 State Hose Champions are pictured here on Whitewater Street, looking north. Frank W. Pratt was the mayor and Howard Salisbury the fire chief. There were three teams in the city, one on the east side near the school, one on Whitewater Street, and one near the high school on Center Street. One hook and ladder truck was stationed near Whitewater Street, too. (Whitewater Fire Department.)

THE HOOK AND LADDER TRUCK IN A JULY 4TH PARADE. This parade photograph dates from the early 1900s, after the hook and ladder truck began to be pulled by horses. The truck is passing by what is now the Hamilton House Bed and Breakfast on Main Street, which has always been a popular spot for watching parades. (Library; Fran Achen Collection.)

THE WATER TOWER. These men are in a precarious position as they work on Whitewater's first water tower, erected in 1889, shortly after the first artesian well had been drilled. At first the reservoir was uncovered and exposed to the elements; later it was covered. This is among the oldest tanks in the United States, and despite its age and small capacity (170,000 gallons), it is still in operation. (Jon Kachel.)

THE WALWORTH HOTEL. The Walworth Hotel on Main Street was erected in 1890; many dignitaries were present at its opening banquet in February 1891, including former Governor William D. Hoard. The house next to the hotel was the residence of Dr. Clark Miller. A Civil War veteran, he was the first of three Dr. Millers to practice in Whitewater; his son Howard and grandson Russell followed in his footsteps. (WHS.)

MORRIS PRATT INSTITUTE. Morris Pratt designed and built what was said to be the first Spiritualist Temple in the world at the corner of Center and Fremont Streets in 1889. In 1902, Pratt donated the temple so that it could become a school. Its president, Moses Hull, crisscrossed the country to raise money to keep the school open. At the start of the Depression, the school closed. Later used as a home for aging spiritualists and a girls' dormitory, it was taken down in 1961. (Author.)

METROPOLITAN HALL. Henry Rile sketched this hall in 1861. Located on the south side of Center Street, it measured 40 feet by 70 feet, could seat 1,000 persons, and was well lit and ventilated. Elections, town meetings, programs, and entertainments were all held here. A fire destroyed the building, along with a complete block on the south side of Center Street, in 1870. (WHS.)

HOSE CHAMPS BANQUET. After the fire, Joseph Bower rebuilt the entire block, which became known as the Bower's Block. The new Bower's Hall, formerly Metropolitan Hall, was located in the middle of the block. Here we see that a lively banquet will take place in 1898, after the Fire Department's State Champion Hose Cart Team won the title. (Whitewater Fire Department.)

SPRINGS NEAR THE DUMP. This scene is not too different when one looks west from the Franklin Street bridge today. The dump was in use up to the end of October 1950. (WHS.)

July 23, 1885 R

Recollections.

Dear REGISTER:—It is a long time since you have heard from me, but you are not quite forgotten. Ill health and the never-ending cares of a large family (of chickens) have occupied my time and thoughts this summer, almost to the exclusion of every other duty which should have claimed a share of my attention.

It is doubtful if I can "recollect" much more that will be very interesting to your readers, but I will try to recall one or two incidents of practical joking which were perpetrated on some of the settlers in the days of "auld lang syne."

I well remember of hearing my brothers, one day, laughing over the discovery of a "salt spring" by a neighbor, (permit him to be nameless,) who lived on the west side of the mill-pond.

Said discovery filled his coffers so suddenly that he immediately erected a gorgeous castle, (in Spain,) ready furnished, the larder filled to overflowing with all the necessaries and luxuries of life, and peopled with a retinue of servants who awaited the commands of the master and mistress.

His castle rose with the speed of Jonah's gourd, without even an examination of the foundation upon which it was built, and, but for a providential interference, I might have been called upon to relate something akin to the dreadful tenement building disaster in New York city. But "interested" friends wished to see the spring; some one suggested that it be cleared of the debris which had been allowed to accumulate in its waters ere their valuable qualities were discovered; which suggestion was forthwith acted upon, when, lo and behold ! among the varied rubbish was found—an old stocking filled with salt ! Alas for that castle ! Great was the fall thereof.

MNEMOSYNE.

A "SALT" SPRING. This is a recollection letter printed in the *Whitewater Register*, July 23, 1885. (*Whitewater Register.*)

WHITEWATER BELL TOWER. This is the junction of Whitewater and Main Streets, looking south. The old wooden bell tower was erected in 1892 to replace a metal triangle, located across the street by the wagon factory, which was used to sound the fire alarm up to that point. The tower was replaced by a steel one in 1898, and when the city hall was about to be built in 1899, this tower and bell were moved to the other side of the street, near the Wisconsin Dairy Supply Company. (WHS; Scholl Collection.)

LAYING THE GROUNDWORK FOR CITY HALL. Notice the work conditions enjoyed in the old days. Note, also, the "bulldozer," used to soften up the ground for loading onto the "four wheelers." How many people wear clothing like this on today's construction sites? Behind them is the Wisconsin Dairy Supply Company, established in 1883, and a few "sidewalk superintendents." (Jon Kachel.)

BUILDING CITY HALL, 1899–1900. There is a lot of history here. The fire bell tower stands in the background, having been moved from its previous location and lowered. A long, narrow shed that stored the fire department's hook and ladder truck, a hose cart, and supplies sits alongside the tower to the left. The large frame warehouse to the right of the tower, across the railroad tracks, stored goods in preparation for shipment by rail. (WHS; Scholl Collection.)

CITY HALL, COMPLETED. This was the heart of the city for 70 years. It housed the city government, police department, and fire department. The City Council met here, a recreation room was later added for those who enjoyed a game of cards, and a library and reading room, along with public restrooms. And, it cannot be forgotten that a small portion of the building was allotted to a jail cell of sorts, for holding miscreants before they were transferred to the county jail. (Author.)

Four

THE MILITARY

COMPANY C. Soldiers deserve a special history of their own to honor the role they played in the nation's wars. In 1859, a unit was formed known as the Lincoln Wide-Awake Brigade. During the Civil War, Whitewater native John J. Downey was one of the youngest soldiers to enter and he served famously as the Drummer Boy of Shiloh. After the war, veterans joined the Charles C. Curtis Post No. 34 of the GAR (Grand Army of the Republic), so named in honor of the man who led the first troops into service in 1861. After the Spanish-American War, an article in the local paper stated that another Whitewater man, Charles A. Jones, was the youngest soldier to have served in the war. The local American Legion Post No. 173 was established in December 1919. In 1924, the American Legion determined that the identity of the youngest soldier in the whole country to serve in World War I was Theodore Hitch, living in Whitewater. In this photograph, proud men pose at Camp Douglas in 1910. (Matt Winn.)

An Honor for the Troops. Emilia Esterly, wife of George Esterly of the Esterly Harvesting Machine Company, made the silk flag pictured below. She presented it to the first contingent of troops that left for service in the Civil War on June 15, 1861. (WHS.)

The Civil War Flag. This flag was carried in all of the Whitewater regiment's campaigns until the end of the war. It was then rolled up and stored and eventually donated to the Whitewater Historical Society. In the 1980s, the historical society joined with the American Legion and the Veterans of Foreign Wars local chapters to have the flag restored and placed in an enclosed case so that visitors could view it. (WHS.)

CIVIL WAR VETERANS. Local photographer Rella Moss took this 1925 photograph of the last 14 members of the Grand Army of the Republic post, the first time each and every member had gathered together in the post's history. From left to right they are (first row) C. N. Griffith, John J. Downey, and Harlan P. Goodman; (second row) A. S. Crescent, Christ Gunderson, G. A. Unkrich, Commander M. W. Parker, A. H. Messerschmidt, John Lean, and Dan Ewing; (third row) John E. Stevens, August S. Anderson, E. H. Wilbut, and Abe Tubbs. (WHS.)

WHITEWATER'S FIRST ARMORY. The Custer Rifles were recruited under orders dated May 19, 1877. Later, the unit became Company C, and its members served in the Spanish-American War, the Mexican Border Patrol, and World War I. For years, the unit tried in vain to find a place to train and meet up. Finally, the second story of the new Van Voorhees Block, on Whitewater Street, was dedicated as the Armory in November 1887. (Library; Fran Achen Collection.)

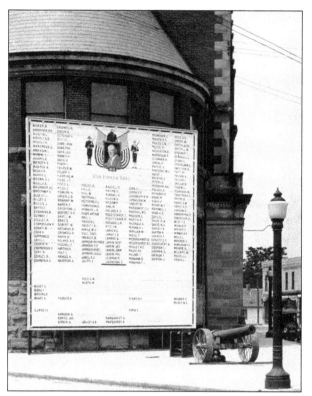

THE WORLD WAR I HONOR ROLL.
In this 1918 photograph, a list of
Whitewater residents who served
in World War I is displayed in
front of the city hall alongside a
Parrott Cannon from the Civil War,
acquired in November 1900. The
cannon was later replaced with a
newer version, which became fodder
for World War II, and the honor roll
sign was removed. The boards from
the sign were recently discovered in
a nearby house, having been used as
floor boards in the attic. (Library;
Fran Achen Collection.)

WAR MEMORIAL EAGLE. This memorial
for all wars was erected on the tip of Flat
Iron Park, or Library Park, in 1922. It
was dedicated on Armistice Day (now
known as Veteran's Day); stores closed
for several hours for the dedication. A
show of unity among the city and its
veterans, it can be viewed by all who
stroll down Main Street today. (WHS.)

THE SECOND ARMORY AND THE WORLD WAR II HONOR ROLL. The armory on North Street was built in 1942 and included the World War II honor roll. The armory was in part a Works Progress Administration (WPA) project; this solidly-built building is still here today. (Author.)

THE BUSY BEE'S SALUTE TO THE TROOPS. This photograph of the popular Busy Bee coffee shop was taken in the fall of 1943 for a special edition of the *Whitewater Register* sent to guardsmen whose unit had been called up in 1940. Pictured here are Howard Winn, Frank Mason, Harry Lowe, Ken Uglow, Jack Kyle, Butch Martin, Robert Coe, Joe Ocasek, R. B. Hellen, Ivy Arnold, Art Kildow, Herb Zabel, Odie O'Donnald, Link Hawes, Curly Chamberlain, Tommy Leonard, George Crumb, Flowy Jolliffe, Ells Coe, Harry Habbard, Ed Jolliffe, and Rue Birch. (Danny Williams.)

THE WHITEWATER RAINCOAT COMPANY. Whitewater had its own version of Rosie the Riveter in the raincoat factory, which employed over 450 people, mostly women, during World War II. The company was established in 1925 and by 1940 was located in the old armory on Whitewater Street. In this photograph, a soldier, Harold Olson, sits on the curb surrounded by the workers. Olson still has breakfast among the "old timers" in town today. (WHS.)

A SALUTE FROM THE STATE GUARD. This photograph appeared in the *Whitewater Register* on October 14, 1943. From left to right, they are Capt. Richard O'Connor, Gordon Saunders, Edward Chady, Joe Ocaseck, LeRoy Douglas, Carl Floerke, Hervy Duerst, Lloyd Sietam, John Schumacher, Joe Kinzer, Tom Anderson, Al Converse, Virgil Graham, Charles Murray, George Albrecht, Ed Benner, Tony Karay, Clarence Peck, Cliff Henderson, Willis Miller, Erv Schimmel. Ed Coe, Harry Tucker, Walt Tratt, John Olsen, Clay Daggett, Frank Mayer, Bill Hall, Bill McLaughlin, Charles Coe, and Lt. Charles Hill. Not pictured is M. Williams. (Author.)

Five

SCHOOLS, CEMETERIES, AND CHURCHES

SIDEWALKS TO THE DOWNTOWN. Early leaders insisted on sidewalk access for residents. The May 7, 1869, issue of the *Whitewater Register* mentions "Sidewalks are to be constructed from Newcomb Street to the downtown." This is the portion along State Street (now east Main Street), near the crest of the hill where Oak Grove Cemetery is located. Just beyond the cemetery is the East Side School. The first log school house in Whitewater was built near the Territorial Oak tree on Main Street in 1840, at the same time the town was getting organized with a post office, a militia, and its first churches. Up the street, the Whitewater Normal School, eventually the University of Wisconsin-Whitewater, was established in 1868. Two cemeteries, Hillside and Calvary, joined Oak Grove as the town grew over the years. Settlers organized churches as early as 1838; eventually Methodist, Unitarian, Congregational, Episcopal, Baptist, Lutheran, and Catholic churches were founded during the 1800s. Some of the city's most notable landmarks are its old church buildings. (Library; Fran Achen Collection.)

A Far-Off View of the Normal School. Ernest L. Hardy, a local photographer, climbed the water tower in Starin Park and took this photograph of the Whitewater Normal School around 1906. The streets around it were not too built up as they had only recently been put through, and the land platted for lots. The main portion of this building, known as Old Main, burned down in 1970. (Author.)

The Normal School, 1911. After it opened in 1868 with 39 students and nine faculty, the Whitewater Normal School gradually increased enrollment, peaking at 600 in 1924. During World War II, enrollment at the school dipped to under 300 and in 1946 rose to nearly 700. The GI Bill was an important factor in the increases in enrollment that followed the war. Current enrollment is over 11,000. (Author.)

WOMEN'S PHYSICAL EDUCATION. Florence Goodhue, shown standing against the wall, was the director of physical education at Whitewater Normal School. She was born and raised in Whitewater, the daughter of postmaster Frank Goodhue, and went to the Normal Training School, graduating in 1915. She later enrolled in several institutions of higher learning and returned to Whitewater in 1922. She lived to see Goodhue Hall named in her honor in 1962, before her death in 1970. (Author.)

NORMAL SCHOOL ASSEMBLY ROOM. Albert Salisbury became the Whitewater Normal School president in 1885. He introduced new curriculum, expanded the reputation of the school, was a leading figure in the Home Coming in 1907, and helped bring the Halverson log cabin to the grounds. The cabin was filled with pioneer artifacts, many of which can be seen at the Whitewater Historical Society Depot Museum today. The school newspaper, the *Royal Purple*, and the yearbook, the *Minnieska*, were founded in 1901 and 1909 respectively, under his tenure. (Author.)

THE EAST SIDE SCHOOL. Erected in 1857, this school has been completely rebuilt over time. In this 1950s photograph, a fire escape slide, which well-behaved students were occasionally allowed to use, is seen on the east side of the school. (Library; Fran Achen Collection.)

STUDENTS AT THE SCHOOL, C. 1906. From left to right, they are (first row) Harold Stone, Lawrence Faust, Harold Brown, Joe Dorr, Arleigh Brown, ? Hefty, and Thayne Savee; (second row) Earl Knecht, Delos Noyes, Walter Selle, Robert Chamberlain, Alvin Taylor, Russell Kutz, Fred Chamberlain, Roy Hall, Arthur Lowery, Arnold Garlock, Otis Wheelock, Ben Weiner, Ralph Henderson, and Raymond "Curly" Chamberlain; (third row) Hazel Perry, Maude Savee, Lillian Miller, Pearl Summers, Etta Selle, Nellie Wheelock, Stella Wintermute, Hazel Peich, May Hansen, Mabel Cadman, Marion Rood, Neva Knecht, and Erma Summers; (fourth row) Truman Millard, Hilda Didrickson, Marjorie Kinney, Adolph Schoechert, Marjorie Dorr, Irene Olsen, Pattie Wintermute, Jessie Campbell, Frances Holmes, Zella House, Izore Johnson, Irma Dutcher, and teacher Edith B. Cary; (fifth row) Principal Charles Hill, teacher Miss Greely, teacher Redella Peich, ? Sweno, Florence Niquet, Gladys Johnson, Lillian Johnson, Ida Johnson, May Summers, Frances Murphy, and Ruth Henderson. (Author.)

BIG BRICK HIGH SCHOOL. This is the replacement for the Old Union School, built in 1883. The first high school program was started here in 1885 and later the building became the Whitewater High School. In January 1928, shortly before students were to move to a brand-new high school, this building burned down. Many high school mementos, especially from the Home Coming year, feature the Big Brick School. (Author.)

BASEBALL CHAMPS. Whitewater has had great teams and athletes throughout the years, these boys were the state baseball champions in 1906. From left to right, they are (first row) Frank Williams, second base; Rollin Whitney, first base; Bert Larkin, substitute; and Stephen E. Dougherty, center fielder; (second row) Harold Anderson, substitute; Alfred Johnson, pitcher; Walter Cox, third base; Archie Anderson, catcher; Lynn Aldrich, substitute; (third row) Earl Cox, left fielder; professor Rittenburg; Art Spangler, short stop; Stephen Burdick, manager; and Clayton Cox, right fielder. (Author.)

THE ESTERLY SCHOOL. The Esterly home at the end of Center Street was sold to the city in August 1894 and used as the west side elementary school until 1927, when it was demolished, and the new high school erected on the site. (Coburn family.)

CITY HIGH SCHOOL. The new high school, built in 1927, was nearly completed when fire destroyed the old high school building, located just down the street. The new school opened its doors a short while after. It not only housed the high school, it housed the elementary students from the old Esterly School it replaced. In the late 1950s, this building became the junior high school. It was abandoned in the 1990s and later demolished. (Author.)

OAK GROVE CEMETERY. James Trippe donated the land for the Oak Grove Cemetery in 1842 and was one of the first interred there in 1844. George Esterly donated the gates, which originally had a stile at the south entrance, in 1884. Here, Fred Kraege (author) stands under the arch in 1991. He compiled records of 31 area cemeteries in and around the city. This is one of the few cemeteries in Wisconsin that can claim two Revolutionary War veterans, three from the War of 1812, and about 40 from the Civil War. (Author.)

HILLSIDE CEMETERY. In 1858, the Cemetery Association purchased about 10 acres on a hill bordering Cravath Lake, across from the downtown. The first lots were sold that fall. The first burial was for Mary Dann in April 1859. In 1894, the original gate and stile were removed and two picturesque columns and an arch were put in. In 1897, a small chapel was erected, and later removed. (Author.)

THE CATHOLIC CHURCH AND CALVARY CEMETERY. Whitewater's Catholic congregation began assembling in the early 1840s, meeting at area homes. In 1853, their first church, pictured here, was opened on Cottage Street, with a rectory added in 1856. This older church was moved in 1873, to the corner of Cottage and High Streets, where it was converted into a school that operated until the fall of 1906, with an average of 90 pupils every year. In 1865, Lucinda and Nelson Fryer deeded four acres of land in Jefferson County for a Catholic cemetery located north of the Whitewater Normal School. In time the school expanded and property was exchanged so that another parcel could be formed. In 1914, a new stone gateway was installed, with a road and a sidewalk to the top of the hill, where the cemetery was located. A subsequent exchange of land with the State of Wisconsin allowed the cemetery to expand, and it was finally fenced in. Today, this cemetery is apparently one of only two private cemeteries located within the boundaries of an American university campus, the other being Kentucky's Bowling Green State University. (St. Patrick's.)

ST. PATRICK'S CATHOLIC CHURCH. This church was dedicated on Cottage Street in May 1867. In 1926, a new rectory and a remodeling of the church were completed, culminating in a celebration commemorating the Diamond Jubilee of the founding of the parish. Once again the church saw its congregation outgrow its building, so land was purchased on the corner of Main and Elizabeth Streets. Construction soon began, and the new church, was dedicated on June 29, 1958. The building pictured was eventually torn down. (St. Patrick's.)

ST. LUKE'S EPISCOPAL CHURCH. Henry Rile sketched this view of St. Luke's Episcopal Church in 1860. The congregation was organized in 1852 and the first frame church built that same year. Renovated in 1867, the church was destroyed by fire in February 1869. (WHS.)

NEW ST. LUKE'S EPISCOPAL CHURCH. Wisconsin's old settlers were a determined group, and the corner stone for a new church was placed in June 1869. The new church was completed less than a year later, on November 3, 1869. It is one of the city's most striking landmarks today. (Author.)

TWO CHURCHES.
Both the Episcopal
Church, erected
in 1869, and the
Congregational
Church, built in
1882, are pictured
on this stereo card
of Church Street.
Stereo cards were a
fad beginning in the
1870s, leaving many
scenes such as this
as a record of the
past. (WHS.)

**THE CONGREGATIONAL
CHURCH.**
The Congregational
Church was organized
in 1840 by Reverend
Daniel Smith and had
15 members. Meetings
were held at various
homes until the first
church in Whitewater,
and the surrounding
countryside, was built in
1843. Immigrants coming
into the village would
often stop in during the
service, after which they
were surrounded by the
members asking, "Where
are you going to settle?"
The advice given to them
was, "Come and settle
here, this is the best
section in the
west!" (WHS.)

THE OLD METHODIST CHURCH. Henry Rile sketched the old Methodist Church in 1859. The society had been organized in 1843 with a membership of 10. This church was erected in 1851 on Church Street and later sold to St. John's Evangelical Lutheran Church in 1872. (WHS.)

THE NEW METHODIST CHURCH. In 1872, a new Methodist Church was built and dedicated on the corner of Center and Prairie Streets. A pipe organ was installed in 1887, and electric lights replaced oil lamps in 1896. It has undergone many improvements throughout the years and is thoroughly a landmark. (WHS.)

THE NORWEGIAN LUTHERAN CHURCH. Ole Bull, a noted Norwegian violinist in the mid-1800s, was asked to come and present a concert in Whitewater. In January 1868, he obliged the good folks. He donated a generous sum ($88) to the Norwegian Lutheran Society, which was used to buy the land on Cravath Street where the church was later built. This distant view of the church, taken for a stereo card, is the only one known to exist. The building was built in 1869, but the congregation was short of funds, so the altar and other furnishings were not installed until 1874. Later, this church was torn down and the lumber used to build a hospital. Seeking a new place of worship for a growing congregation, the Norwegian Lutherans purchased the Baptist church, on the corner of Fourth and Main Streets, in 1908. (WHS.)

LAYING THE CORNERSTONE FOR THE BAPTIST CHURCH. The Baptist Church was organized in 1842 and held services at various locations in the early years. In 1886, the cornerstone of the Baptist Church was set in place on the corner of Fourth and Main Streets. (WHS.)

THE BAPTIST CHURCH. The Baptist Church was not completed until 1887, due to the lack of funding. In 1908, the Baptists sold the church to the Norwegian Lutherans. In 1898, a paragraph in *Whitewater of To-day* stated, "It has been suggested that the seating capacity of Whitewater churches is so large that should every man, woman, and child of the City desire to attend church at the same hour, there would be a seat for each one." (Library; Fran Achen Collection.)

THE NORWEGIAN LUTHERAN CHURCH. The Norwegian Lutheran Church on the east side was used for about 40 years, until the Baptist church was purchased. No great change was made to its structure for many years. The church was affiliated with other Norwegian Lutheran Churches at Skoponong, Heart Prairie, and Sugar Creek, but they separated in 1932. Services were held in both Norwegian and English. (Author.)

THE FIRST ENGLISH LUTHERAN CHURCH. In 1937, the Norwegian Lutheran Church changed its name to the First English Lutheran Church. Its membership has steadily grown, and the church underwent a major addition in 2000. It is a prominent landmark today. (Library; Fran Achen Collection.)

OLD ST. JOHN'S LUTHERAN CHURCH. The early history of St. John's Evangelical Lutheran Church is uncertain. The German Lutherans began holding services in schools and public halls around 1853. In 1865, they acquired their first building, and in 1872, the old Methodist church was purchased. This building was remodeled in 1885, and used until the new church was built on the same site in 1925. (St. John's.)

NEW ST. JOHN'S LUTHERAN CHURCH. When the old church ended its term of serving its members, it was said that it was, at 75 years of age, the oldest public building in Whitewater. The new church was dedicated March 22, 1925. (St. John's.)

UNION SCHOOL AND THE UNIVERSALIST CHURCH. The old Union School was in service until 1883, when it was almost completely demolished and a new school erected on the site, using some materials from the old building. In 1885, it was the location of the area's first high school. Until this time, the academic department at the Whitewater Normal School had been considered superior for students who wanted a secondary education. (WHS.)

THE UNIVERSALIST CHURCH. The Universalist Church cornerstone was laid in 1868, and the church dedicated in 1869. It was on the corner of Center and Prairie Streets, opposite the Methodist church and across Prairie Street from the old Union School and the high school. Lightening hit the church in 1902. In the 1920s, it served as a luncheon room for Whitewater Normal School students. It was finally destroyed by fire in 1928. (WHS.)

MAIN STREET, 1864. This view of Main Street shows the old gristmill on the right and the Montour House hotel looming over it. The first sets of brick buildings covered two-thirds of the south side. The wooden stores and hotel in the first block beyond the mill were destroyed by fire in 1867 and gradually rebuilt. (WHS.)

MAIN STREET, 1907. This view in 1907, from a greater distance, shows the heart of the city—city hall. The addition to the rear of the original gristmill appears similar to the Montour House and was built by Julius Birge's father in 1856. As in 1907, when one comes into town from the east today, the roof tops on the south side of the street are similar to that in 1864. (Author.)

Six

THE FARMERS' TOWN

HAULING GRAIN TO TOWN. In this photograph, Seymour Blunt leads a group of his farmer neighbors from south of the city into town on Franklin Street with wagonloads of grain. After the loss of two large manufacturers—the wagon company and the harvesting machine company—Whitewater's economy largely depended on agriculture, commerce, and the growing Whitewater Normal School. Of these, the farmer's trade was the mainstay. Railroads shipped grain and produce and brought farm machinery in return. Whitewater Street (once known as Railroad Street) was a bustling hive of agricultural-related activity. Nearby, many small commercial businesses worked to boost the welfare of the city and its inhabitants. The farm economy remained strong in Whitewater after World War II, when the railroad ruled and the farmers' trips into the city were frequent, benefiting downtown businesses. But after the railroad era, trucks came directly to the farmers, allowing them to transfer their goods to rural warehouses and storage facilities, rather than coming into town. After World War II, the normal school became a college, with many more students enrolled. It eventually replaced industry and agriculture as the city's economic leader, and today is its largest employer. (Author.)

DEPOT AND FREIGHT HOUSE. This is a view of the depot and freight house taken in the 1890s by local photographer H. P. Goodman for the *Whitewater of To-day* booklet. The depot, built in 1890, stood for nine years before the Whitewater sign was placed on its roof after local townsmen asked for it. A livery wagon waits to take passengers and baggage to their final destination. (Author.)

THE RAILROAD YARDS NORTH OF THE DEPOT. The railroad was a great asset to the village when it started regular service in January 1853. Warehouses sprang up all along Whitewater Street, along with stores, a meat packing plant, and a grain elevator. When the manufacturing plants were here, there was a switch engine to shift cars from the Red Mill on the west side and the Esterly Harvesting Machine Company on the east side. Whitewater was a bustling city in those days. (Library; Fran Achen Collection.)

THE THRESHING MACHINE TRAIN. This train, on the rails near the Whitewater depot in 1900, carried J. I. Case harvesting machines and other farm equipment. It made several annual runs from Racine to the western wheat fields during the summer. There is a logo of "Old Abe," the Civil War Eagle of fame, on the front. Schulte's Brass Band, of Racine, accompanied it with inspirational music. This was the fifth train of its type that summer. (Library; Fran Achen Collection.)

THE RAILROAD STATION, 1907. The railroad station was a busy scene of passengers and freight. In the early days, it was met by the stage going to Fort Atkinson and a livery for local service. On the right are the buildings on the west side of Whitewater Street. At this time there was only one grain elevator near the depot and small businesses along the street near the rails. (Author.)

THE RAILWAY EXPRESS OFFICE. Howard Winn (left) and an unidentified employee stand in the Railway Express Office on Whitewater Street in 1918. The office was located in various stores in town until finally ending up in the vicinity of the depot and the freight house. (Matt Winn.)

A BUSTLING OFFICE. The office was a busy place when the farmers were carrying the city. Besides old office equipment in the picture, from left to right are Harry Prechel, driver; Bill Blake, driver; and Howard Winn, agent. (Matt Winn.)

FREIGHT WAGONS. These freight wagons are loaded with veal calves waiting to be shipped to market. The farmers' trade amounted to about 66 percent of the demand among the city's businessmen. Pictured here from left to right are Harry Prechel (driver), Howard Winn (agent), Ed Winn (clerk), and William Blake (driver). A corner of the Dadmun Mill can be seen in the left-hand side of the photograph. (Matt Winn.)

READY FOR SHIPMENT. This view from the other side of the rails shows the Dadmun elevator in the background. On the back of this postcard was written "Dear Sir, Hear [sic] is a picture I would like you to put in the Messenger, a shipment of calves from Edgewood Farm, Orie Coburn proprietor. And in the month of April 1913 we shipped out over 500 calves. Yours truly, agent F. R. Pierson." (Matt Winn.)

THE B LINE THAT NEVER WAS. Ever since the first rail line reached Whitewater in 1852, some businessmen tried to get a rail line from Chicago to the northwest, but never succeeded. The last effort was in 1914, when the connection to Whitewater could not be completed due to a lack of funds. This is the first car of that B line, perhaps the only photograph of its kind. (Kettwig family.)

A WRECK ON EAST SIDE. This picture shows a derailed freight engine that smashed into a building of the Minnesota Lumber Company on a spur leading to the old paper mill (later the location of the condensery) on the city's east side. People enjoyed being "sidewalk superintendents" when these accidents occurred. (Author.)

TRAIN OVER THE BRIDGE. This is the milk train that headed east to Milwaukee after the beginning of the 20th century. In the morning it stopped at every station on the line exchanging mail, baggage, and passengers. In the evening, the train rushed through, unless flagged down to allow one or more passengers to board at small rural villages. These were known as whistle stops. (Lawrence Taylor family.)

THE LAST PASSENGER TRAIN OUT OF TOWN. This is one of local photographer Walt Peterson's most famous pictures, the last passenger train out of Whitewater on November 29, 1951. The engine, a diesel-electric, started its service on the line in the late 1920s. It made this trip east to Milwaukee during the day and in the evenings headed west. (Author.)

WEYHER BLACKSMITH AND WAGON SHOP. This shop was located on the corner of Fourth and Whitewater Streets. Theodore Weyher learned the trade in Prussia and immigrated to Wisconsin (after serving in the war against Denmark), finally settling in Whitewater in 1895. His son Edward became a partner and after 1900 invented an improved wagon and began making and selling them at his shop on the corner of Ann and Trippe Streets, next to the railroad. (Henry Meisner.)

THE CANNING FACTORY. A group of local businessmen purchased the interests of the wagon shop in 1910 and converted it into a canning factory that began operating in 1914, canning corn. Later, peas and tomatoes were also canned, and up to 140 people were employed when the harvest was in full swing. This was in the heyday of the farmer and cash cropping with vegetables. (WHS.)

THE LARGE ICEHOUSE. Myer and Maier of Milwaukee started to build this mammoth icehouse in the fall of 1898, but were soon accused of shipping the ice out of town at a huge profit. City leaders objected and assessed a tax on the ice; by 1902 the icehouse was being dismantled. It had the name Knickerbocker Ice Company at the time. There were about 10 different icehouses in the city throughout the years, harvesting ice from the lakes. (Author.)

A GASOLINE-POWERED ICE SAW. Claude "Dude" Fero (left) and a partner pose with a gasoline-powered saw during a break on Cravath Lake. Running along on tubular runners, this machine may have made the snow fly, but it sure saved the huff and puff of using the ice saw. The brewery, Union Produce, the railroad, and area dairies all had their icehouses to fill, and there were various individuals who filled their own icehouses and sold ice to residents. (Russ Fero.)

UNLOADING GRAIN. After the Esterly Harvesting Machine Company was razed and the site vacant for years, the Badgerland Co-op opened its doors for business on the property on February 1, 1935. A gas station and grain storage silos were the first steps towards a large facility that served farmers. Here, unloading grain from the back of a pickup are, from left to right, Ed Hoffman, Merle Brigham, Harold Vail, Frank Kligora, and an unidentified man. (Coburn family.)

CO-OP
FEEDS
FROM MILLS YOU OWN
MIDLAND COOPERATIVE WHOLESALE

THE FINISHED PRODUCT. After the grain is ground and nutrients are added, it is bagged and then tied and loaded for home. In this photograph from left to right are unidentified, unidentified, Don Emmer, William Drays, unidentified, and Frank Hesselman. The Badgerland Co-op later moved to a site west of Whitewater, this first site is now the home of the Eastsider, with its gas pumps and convenience store. (Coburn family.)

Seven

THE EARLY 1900S

City Hall from the Lake, Whitewater, Wis.

41328.

VIEW ACROSS THE LAKE. This c. 1900 photograph was taken from a point on the shore of Cravath Lake in Hillside Cemetery looking toward the downtown and the heart of the city—city hall. This was a period of giving back to the city, in gratitude for the past. City hall was built in 1900, and it became a cherished landmark in Whitewater. In 1903, Julius Birge, the first settler-child born in Whitewater, donated the Birge Fountain in appreciation of the city of his birth. In 1904, a generous donation was given for the erection of the new library near the fountain. The next year, 1905, the stately Masonic temple was built. In 1906, the Whitewater Federation of Women's Clubs published, which provided much of the information used in this book. It was a written history of the founding of the city. To round out this period, the greatest event ever held in the city occurred in 1907, the Home Coming. This four-day event, which featured parades and public celebration, was truly a community effort, the likes of which the city had never seen since. (Matt Winn.)

WHITEWATER'S BOOSTER. Iram Z. Merriam, a local businessman, came to Whitewater after employment in Iowa and Fort Atkinson. He was a salesman for the Esterly Harvesting Machine Company and in the shops he invented and patented related products, including the instant slat repair kit, which became very successful. Merriam and John Burton, who ran Whitewater's main real estate business, were instrumental in publishing this first history pamphlet of Whitewater in 1898, entitled *Whitewater of To-day.* (Cleon Newton.)

WHITEWATER OF TO-DAY. In 1898, the authors, J. E. Burton and I. Z. Merriam, wrote: "To the citizens of Whitewater by whose aid this work was made a possible success, and into whose hands the future of our beautiful city is placed, with the hope that the same spirit of enterprise, pluck, and liberality, which they have shown in the past, will in the near future place Whitewater in the front rank of American inland cities, this work is respectfully dedicated by the authors."

A Holiday Parade at First and Main Streets. This is the corner of what was then known as the Chamberlain Block, built in the early 1860s. The First National Bank of Whitewater opened its doors in 1863 on the lower level. In the 1890s, the bank put a new front on the lower level of the building. The former bank is now a restaurant, but the door of the original bank vault can be seen there today. The Citizens National Bank was founded in 1883 in the second block of Main Street, on the south side. It reorganized in 1893 and a year later merged with the First National Bank, but each maintained separate quarters until 1931, when they reorganized as the First Citizens State Bank. (Library; Fran Achen Collection.)

JULIUS C. BIRGE
(THE FIRST WHITE CHILD BORN IN WHITEWATER)

IN APPRECIATION. Julius C. Birge was the first white child born in the new settlement, on November 18, 1839. His father, William, bought the stone mill in 1853 and added the brick addition to it in 1856. He died in 1860, and Julius, who was 20, successfully ran the mill until illness forced him to go west. He later returned to St. Louis, where he formed the Semple and Birge Manufacturing Company. He was also vice-president of the Winchester & Partridge Manufacturing Company. (WHS.)

THE BIRGE FOUNTAIN. Julius Birge presented this fountain to the city of his birth on July 4, 1903. At that time, it was one of the largest fountains in the county, and there was some consternation among city officials about how much water it would require. It was placed on the site where the "Little Brick" schoolhouse, which Julius Birge attended as a child, was erected in 1844. (Author.)

MARY FLAVIA WHITE.
Judge Samuel A. White was
appointed to the board of
Whitewater Normal School
regents in 1865 and led the
effort to bring the normal
school to Whitewater in
1868. He moved here with
his wife and seven children.
One of them, Mary Flavia,
later bequeathed a sum of
money to the city to build a
library that would be located
near downtown, as a token of
affection for her childhood
days in the village. (Library.)

WHITE MEMORIAL LIBRARY. The White Memorial Library was dedicated on June 17, 1904. Until this time the library was located in a succession of buildings and rooms downtown. Mary Flavia White's generosity allowed for a fine new building that was open more hours to serve the community. This was the library's home for nearly 90 years, until the Young family donated money for a new building, the Irvin L. Young Memorial Library. (Author.)

THE MASONIC TEMPLE. The Masonic temple was dedicated July 4, 1905, the 50th year since local Masons formed St. John's Lodge, No. 57. The 100th anniversary of this distinguished building, located on the city's main thoroughfare and still in use, was in 2005. (Library; Scholl Collection.)

EARLY

ANNALS OF WHITEWATER

1837-1867

WRITTEN BY

PROSPER CRAVATH, ESQ.

1837-1857

Continued by SPENCER S. STEELE, 1857-1867

Edited by ALBERT SALISBURY, 1906

Published by

THE WHITEWATER FEDERATION OF
WOMEN'S CLUBS

1906

EARLY ANNALS OF WHITEWATER. This book, a compilation of accounts from as early as 1858 published by the Whitewater Federation of Women's Clubs, has been an invaluable source of information on early Whitewater. In the Foreword, its editor, Albert Salisbury, is commended for his work done "not for possible compensation, but for love of his native community and a desire to commemorate the persons and events, which made Whitewater one of the most attractive towns in Wisconsin." Salisbury himself writes, in his Preface, "I, who reach from the first generation of settlers in this vicinity over into the third generation, have greatly appreciated this privilege of gathering up and setting in order such material as was accessible to me for future reference by all interested in . . . our beloved Whitewater." (WHS.)

ALBERT SALISBURY. One of Whitewater's foremost citizens, Albert Salisbury, was born January 24, 1843. He was educated in a small country school, attended Milton College, became the president of the Brodhead, Wisconsin, schools, and was eventually tapped to become the Whitewater Normal School's president. He attended a Home Coming celebration in Brodhead in 1906 that was so successful that he immediately planned to have one the next year in Whitewater. (Author.)

THE HOME COMING ENVELOPE OF 1907. Albert Salisbury proposed the idea to city leaders upon his return, and a great deal of planning followed. Invitations for the gala event were sent out to former residents, business leaders, students, laborers, and generally anyone associated with the city in some way or another. In the end, approximately 2,000 former residents came back, from nearly every state in the Union, a great show of unity and common purpose among the community. (Author.)

THE HOME COMING PARADE ON MAIN STREET. At the head of the parade was a band, closely followed by members of the Custer Rifles, then the Grand Army of the Republic (Civil War veterans), then the Spanish-American War veterans, and finally the honored speakers in carriages. Far down the street you can see a banner with the words, "Should Auld Acquaintance Be Forgot," which was the theme of the event. (WHS.)

THE NORMAL SCHOOL FLOAT IN THE PARADE. This float, drawn by four white horses abreast, was made up in royal purple and white, the school colors, and carried about 20 similarly dressed young ladies. It was said that this was the most ornate entry in the nearly hour-long parade. (WHS.)

THE HOME COMING PARADE. The parade entries were colorfully adorned. There was a lawn contest held to view the best kept lawns in the city. Parades were always a well-attended attraction. Warren Merrill is pictured driving his Ford, along with Uncle Late Taft and an unknown child in the front seat. In back was "Aunt Louise," Warren's wife; daughter Catherine; Julia Mulks; Aunt Addie; and William Mulks, sitting on the floor. (WHS.)

THE OLD LOG HOUSE.

THE LOG CABIN. Albert Salisbury was always planning ahead. Inspired by the Home Coming in Brodhead, he advertised for a log cabin and any pioneer artifacts that could be acquired for preservation. It did not happen in time for the Home Coming, but the Halverson log cabin was soon reassembled on the Whitewater Normal School lawn and dedicated in the fall of 1907. (Author.)

THE HOSPITAL. The Norwegian Lutheran Church was first located on Cravath Street but later abandoned. It was sold to Charles Martin, who dismantled it and built this hospital with the wood. The hospital was destroyed by fire in January 1925, and today the modern city water tower is found on the site. (Author.)

THE POST OFFICE. The Whitewater Post Office was established in 1840. In the 19th century, most post offices were found in stores, often owned by the postmaster; Whitewater was no exception. David Powers, the first post master, walked to Troy weekly to pick up the mail (a distance of some 20 miles each way). Starting in January 1853, mail was brought by train. When the train stopped running in 1952, temporary trucking service was provided until 1966, when the Highway Postal Service was formed. In 1935, the Federal Government authorized the construction of a post office building on Center Street; now it is the heart of the downtown. (Author.)

Eight

SCENES OF YESTERYEAR

THE BUSY BEE. The calendar on the wall, from the Winchester Hardware store across the street, shows May 1947. The owner, Floyd "Kewpie" Joliffe, keeps his eyes trained on a friendly and loyal "mob." Eddie Skiningsrude (far left) is holding a cup of coffee. Already, some people were gathering memories of Whitewater, in picture and in word, to share with future generations. In 1946, Henry Rile's sketches were donated to the Whitewater Historical Society. In 1986, his autobiography was donated, greatly adding to the understanding of Whitewater's early years. Starting in the mid-1900s, a local photographer named Fran Achen quietly began to develop prints, producing early images of our town that many had never seen, tapping into a c. 1900 collection of glass plate negatives taken by amateur photographer Henry Scholl. This is a medley of scenes, containing photographs from personal collections that are not found in the files of the historical society or the library. (Danny Williams family.)

THE OCTAGON HOUSE. The Octagon House, located on Newcomb Street, was built in the 1860s by Lyman Wight, who also designed and built many of its furnishings. Wight was employed by the Esterly Harvesting Machine Company nearby and was an inventor of a seeder that could be attached to a cultivator, a grain drill, and a corn planter. He also secured a patent on a spinning wheel, which he sold to a manufacturer in Jefferson County. (Library.)

THE HENDERSON HOUSE. A local merchant, A. S. Kinnie, built this house in 1859. Odie Ewing taught high school classes here for 12 students in the 1880s, prior to the establishment of the first high school in 1885. William Wight and his wife lived here until his death in 1911 and hers in 1918. Her daughter, Venetta Chambers Henderson, purchased the home in 1908, and it has been in the Henderson family ever since. (Author.)

A Rile Sketch of the Wright House. This is a Rile sketch of Simon D. Wright's residence, built in 1857, at 302 South Prince Street. He was the leading monument maker in Whitewater, and his name is found throughout the Oak Grove Cemetery. His son, Simon Wright Jr., was Henry Rile's brother-in-law; he and his wife (Rile's sister) Augusta (Gussie) moved to the east for the remainder of their lives. (WHS.)

The Wright House. This photograph shows the yellow brick house as it is today. Simon Wright died in 1867, the same year that Rile completed the above sketch. Rile sketched the back of the same house in 1869, so he must have returned to follow up on unfinished work. (Alan Luckett.)

THE MULKS HOUSE. The Daniel Mulks home is on Fremont Street. In the horse-and-buggy days a carriage barn, or house, was often times located on the premises. The land behind the barn is open, but a few years later, Esterly Avenue, North Franklin, and Park Streets were platted and filled with a dense group of homes. The three streets run to Starin Road, while Fremont Street runs to the north out of town. (Beatrice Mulks Jacobs.)

FARMER'S STORE. William Farmer had this 24-foot-by-40-foot structure (far right) erected on the corner of North and Newcomb streets in 1871, thinking that the railroad running from the south to north was a sure thing; he planned for it to be used as quarters for visitors stopping in when the rails came in. When the B line, the north-south train, was not built, the building was used as a rooming house and, much later, served as Lane's Grocery. (WHS.)

SNOW ON FIRST STREET. This photograph, from the early 1900s, was taken on the east side of First Street, looking north. Weren't the "snow blowers" of that day something special? This is a piece of good operating equipment that uses no gasoline. (Author.)

MORE SNOW ON FIRST STREET. This photograph was taken from the opposite side of the street, looking north. Those were the days of the sleigh and the bobsled. Often times, sleigh rides were special news items in the dailies to inspire good reading material. (Author.)

ED MILLER AND DR. FOWLER'S DOG. This is Ed Miller with Dr. Fowler's dog "standing out," or "out standing," on the sidewalk around 1910. They did not have snow blowers back then yet, and if they did, they probably still would have shoveled by hand. (Author.)

KKK FUNERAL. In the mid-1920s, the Ku Klux Klan attracted a number of members in the area. They operated primarily as a fraternal group in Wisconsin, but did engage in at least one cross burning in Whitewater. In 1925, one of their members, a local deputy sheriff named A. J. Gilbertson, was found dead on a church lawn. Some thought it was murder, but the coroner said it was natural death, probably a heart attack. The controversial death drew Klan members in full regalia to Whitewater for the funeral. The newspaper, in its coverage, commented, "it was an unusual spectacle in Whitewater." Shortly after this, Klan activity died out in the area. (WHS.)

THE NOVELTY BARN. After the Exchange Hotel was dedicated in 1842, a livery stable was located behind it. After the coming of the automobile, the old barn was partitioned off and became known as the Novelty Barn; one of the small shops located in it was Savee's Shoe Shop, later sold to Earl Hunt around 1930. Two of his employees Clifton Henderson and Ralph Kling are shown here. (Author.)

FUN HUNTERS FLOAT. The Fun Hunters were first mentioned in *Early Annals of Whitewater* in 1858, described as boys who grabbed bag and baggage and headed to Lake Koshkonong "for a good time." It seemed their old boats, the *Clementine* and the *Fun Huntress*, got the most raves as being "leaky and unsinkable." Later, Blackhawk Island, Green Lake, and Lauderdale Lake became choice getaway territory. Their last stern wheeler, the *Ark*, paddled Lauderdale Lake. (WHS.)

CONDENSERY. The Whitewater Condensery was located on the site of the old paper mill, which had replaced a burned-out sawmill in 1859. It proved its value to the farmers by providing steady income and to the local economy by providing jobs. It was later acquired by the American Milk Company, and then, in 1944, the Hawthorn Mellody Company. Due to the consolidation in the dairy industry, the company closed this plant in 1992, and the building was taken down in 1999. (WHS.)

RECEIVING ROOM AT THE NEW CONDENSERY. At first, milk was brought to the dairy on wagons, then later, men who owned trucks went from farm to farm and brought the milk in. This also gave the economy a boost, as the farmers were free to stay at home after chores, the milk haulers acquired a seven-day-a-week job, and the milk company gave employment to many men throughout the years. (WHS.)

THE WASHROOM. This view inside the condensery shows the washroom, with Henry James standing by the tank on the right. By the paddles on the left center is Clarence Lurvey. This picture was taken by local photographer W. C. Ralph, who had an office on Center Street near the city hall. (WHS.)

DUNHAM AND FISKE. In a 1916 account in the *Whitewater Register*, this business, located in a portion of the old wagon factory buildings on Whitewater Street, was an important retailer in Whitewater. John Deere and International Harvester farm machinery, windmills and pumps, Cushman binder engines, Titan gas engines, and the Roswell silo filler were all part of the inventory, everything farmers needed in those days. The firm was also an agent for Paige and Dodge automobiles. (Kettwig family.)

THE WHITEWATER GARAGE. The garage was located on Second Street, next door to the corner Armory Building. E. M. Drewry and W. E. Gnatzig were the owners; they were in business at least in 1926 and 1927 and also had a garage in Palmyra. (Library; Fran Achen Collection.)

INSIDE THE GARAGE. The interior of the garage in the days when automobiles were a novelty, and yes, these same cars would be a novelty today, too. There are car buffs who love their old relics. They don't drag race, they handle them with tender loving care. (WHS.)

THE JOLLIFFE AND CHAMBERLAIN FLOAT. A Jolliffe and Chamberlain float is seen in a parade around 1920. There were a lot of merchants in those days, and participation in parades and other civic events was strong. This was in front of the post office when it was located on the corner of First and Main Streets, on the northeast side. (Danny Williams family.)

JOLLIFFE AND CHAMBERLAIN STOREFRONT. Floyd Jolliffe and Fred Chamberlain went into the clothing and furnishings business in 1919, shortly after World War I. The store was on Main Street, and Jolliffe's interest soon turned to that of managing the Busy Bee in the middle of the block. Overseas, Jolliffe wrote home from a hospital and said he sorely missed the pies and sweets back home. (Danny Williams family.)

107

READY FOR CUSTOMERS. Just when Floyd Jolliffe opened the Busy Bee is uncertain, but he had the business for about 30 years. It probably was the most popular spot downtown for the men-folk. There were a few card tables and pool tables in the back, and a few notions were carried, along with a variety of supplies. So popular was this "hive," it carried the moniker of the Madhouse and the Bucket of Blood. Oh! For that togetherness today! (Danny Williams family.)

THE MEN'S DOMAIN. On another occasion, this photograph was taken from the back, looking toward the front door and the assembly area. A few folks line the counter, and a card game is in full swing toward the front. Note there are no ladies present. A standing (if unwritten and unspoken) rule barred ladies from the men's domain. It was probably broken a few times. (Danny Williams family.)

THE MADHOUSE. See the full counter! See the expression of happiness and willingness to share a pose for the cameraman. Behind the counter is Floyd Jolliffe, the proprietor, who bore the nickname of "Kewpie" because of his heavy dark eyebrows. Perhaps one of our readers can identify some of these "busy bees." Look at the photograph on page 57, taken during World War II; most of the men in that picture are in these photographs, taken a few years later. (Danny Williams family.)

CARDS AND KIBITZING. Card tables were filled, and kibitzers would pull up a chair and peer over a player's shoulder, muse about the action, and then have fun discussing it later. Men from every walk of life enjoyed this haven for socializing with friends. It mattered not if they were in a business vying against each other; this was a friendly alliance. "All the world's a stage, and its players merely actors." The play is over. Back again tomorrow. (Danny Williams family.)

JOSEPH BOWER. Joseph C. Bower left his trademark on the city's streets. He came to the village in 1846, after learning the mason's trade in Milwaukee for several years, and helped build the brewery and constructed many of the brick buildings in town. At one time he owned 12 of them. An entire block on the south side of Center Street had been destroyed by fire in 1870, and after he rebuilt it, it was known as Bower's Block. He served many years as town treasurer. (WHS.)

CENTER STREET. This is an early photograph of Center Street, showing a block of small business ventures. Gradually individual brick blocks were built, and new stores made it a busy shopping area. This street headed west to the Esterly School, about nine blocks away. There were no supermarkets in those days, so many merchants competed with one another for trade. (Author.)

THE ICE SKATING RINK. The skating rink was once located downtown, on the old Mill Race, below its dam, between Main and North streets, near where the new skate park is located today. The Klinger Brewery is located on the hill to the right and the North Street bridge below it. (WHS.)

THE OLD SWIMMING HOLE. This is the same site in the summer, looking on from the south end of the pool. The main difference in this picture is that there are only boys in it, as the boys and the girls swam on alternating days. A playground was located on the right of the pool, and many events were held on its grounds throughout the years. The barn at the back of the photograph used to be located on Jefferson Street. (WHS.)

J. C. Coxe Delivery Truck. J. C. Coxe's grocery store was a long-standing asset to the community. By 1916, he had been in the business for 35 years. A larger-than-normal stock of goods was kept, including automobile tires, cigarettes and cigars, and candles. He had two motorized trucks and four wagons for delivery. Claude "Dude" Fero was one of the delivery men for the company. (Russ Fero.)

Fone Fish for Food. E. L. Fish entered the grocery business with a store known as the Quality Grocery. Energetic and progressive, he built up a business that accommodated his customers, was active in community affairs, and added a touch of humor to the town with his slogan, "Fone Fish For Food," which was found on his trucks, in his advertisements, and on receipts from his store. Dude Fero drove this truck, too. (Russ Fero.)

O'CONNOR'S DRUG STORE. This shows the interior of Richard O'Connor's drug store, located on the south side of Main Street. He came to Whitewater in 1846 and ran the drug store and various other business ventures, and was responsible for encouraging sidewalks, planting trees, and beautifying the village and the cemeteries. His sons Fred and Harry J. carried on the drug store business for many years. (WHS.)

THE WHITEWATER LUMBER COMPANY. In 1883, the Minnesota Lumber Company set up their shop at the junction of Wisconsin and Milwaukee Streets, formerly the Trippe estate. A large force of men put in a siding to serve it and the paper mill just to the south. In 1892, it was sold and renamed the Whitewater Lumber Company. It was again sold in the early 1960s, and Donald Hale, the manager at this time, left with all of his crew to begin today's Home Lumber Company. The photograph dates from 1902. (Library; Fran Achen Collection.)

THE EXCAVATION ON HARPER STREET. Besides awkward equipment (compared to today's modern machines), a lot of man power was needed. The city has many areas where limestone lies just beneath the topsoil, and those areas needed to be dynamited before utilities could be placed beneath the surface. These excavations were subject to caving in. (Author.)

INSTALLING SEWER AND WATER ON HARPER STREET. Here is a view of one of the rigs used to install sewer and water mains on Harper Street in the 1940s. This is in front of the Clifton Henderson residence; the sidewalk on the right leads to Gault Street and the Walter Carlson home. (Author.)

WHITEWATER STREET, BEFORE 1910. The west side of the street was lined with small businesses, hotels, grocery stores, barber shops, and saloons. In the distance stands the new city hall. The Dadmun elevator and feed mill sits on the right, the largest in the area and a great attraction for the farmers. This large vacant lot was for the freight house business, as much trade came in and went out through its doors. The elevator was destroyed by fire in the 1960s. (Author.)

LOOKING WEST ON WHITEWATER STREET. All the farmers' needs were met here, with the wagon and blacksmith shops, the depot and freight house, warehouses, the largest elevator and gristmill in the city, and a lumber yard at the far end. There were also two hotels and a variety of merchants supplying groceries, hardware, and other goods that catered to all. This is an early morning view, with the shadows still in the street. (Author.)

MAIN STREET, BEFORE 1917. Peace and quiet reign on this block of Main Street. There were large awnings on the stores on the north side as "Old Sol" and his sidekick, "rays," did damage to the displays in the windows. This is prior to 1917, before the street was paved with bricks. (Author.)

MAIN STREET WHITEWATER WISC 451

MAIN STREET, AFTER 1917. Another view when the old Model Ts were lining the streets as well as a few of the remains of "Old Dobbin" (an affectionate term for a horse) telling us he was still around. This scene was after 1917, and the installation of the brick street was complete. (Author.)

THE COMMERCIAL BANK. This photograph, taken in the 1950s, shows the south side of Main Street. On the corner is the Commercial and Savings Bank, which opened its doors in 1913. During the Great Depression, President Roosevelt declared a national bank holiday in March 1933. The Commercial Bank was ready to reopen before its neighbor, the First Citizen's State Bank. In a show of unity and mutual respect, Commercial Bank officers decided to delay their reopening for one day, so that the two banks could open together. (Jon Kachel; Fran Achen photograph.)

RANDOLPH THE ROOSTER. Walt Peterson took this well-known picture of Randolph crossing Main Street by the library in 1965. Picked up by the wire services, the photograph ran in print around the country. It was even featured in the May 1965 issue of *Life* magazine, with the rooster incorrectly identified as "Rudolph." Randolph was a celebrity in his day, on display at the Walworth County Fair and eventually cared for in a coop south of town. (Tom Barnes.)

COUSIN OTTO. Whitewater resident Gene "Cousin Otto" Lee has been a professional clown for about 70 years. Before coming to Whitewater 54 years ago, he had traveled with three major circuses. He has been a stand-in clown at the Circus World Museum in Baraboo, Wisconsin, and has entertained children and adults at the Walworth County Fair for years on end. He was inducted into the International Clown Hall of Fame in 1992. Call it "Jus' clownin' 'round." (Author.)

THE CLOWN NEWSPAPER. Gene Lee started the *Three Ring News*, now in its 30th year of publication. It was the first clown newspaper in the world. Created for clowns living in the Midwest, subscribers are from all over the United States and overseas. Lee is its only editor, and it includes stories and features just "for the clowns." (Gene Lee.)

THE STONE QUARRY. The stone quarry south of town on Franklin Street has a long history. Numerous owners, workmen, and teamsters have hauled and loaded the crushed stone for our village streets. For the Home Coming of 1907, the city macadamized some streets with limestone. (Library; Fran Achen Collection.)

THE BRICK YARD. Brick yards played an important role in Whitewater's history. As early as May 1841, William Wood had his first kiln on the mill pond south of the railroad tracks, where red bricks were produced. George Dann started another brick works on Cravath Street in 1847, Albert Kendall founded one on Fremont Street in 1852, and A. Y. Chamberlain another one in 1866 that also produced drain tile. Others followed throughout the years, ending with the Brick and Tile Company, which operated on the north side of town from 1903 until the 1940s. (Library; Fran Achen Collection.)

The Original Central Block and Marsh Stores. This shows the center of Block Nine on the south side of Main Street. The large stores on the left were built in 1856 by William Birge, James Worm, and O. P. Conger. The single store on the right was built by Sanger Marsh in 1855. Here we find the shops of H. S. Shedd, D. S. Cook, and Day and O'Connor's Drug Store. (Library; Fran Achen Collection.)

Halverson and Doolittle Storefronts. The Halverson Brothers clothing store began in 1861, and by 1916 it was said to be the largest clothing store between Milwaukee and Madison. It had suits, overcoats, hats and caps, and a popular tailoring service. Ira Doolittle began making and selling shoes in the mid-1880s. On the right of the photograph is the Old Stone Mill, built in 1839, and the fire tower, which was used to raise the fire hose to dry it out. (Library; Fran Achen Collection.)

CORNERSTONE OF OLD CITY HALL. When the cornerstone was set in place for city hall in 1899, a box of historical documents, clippings from local newspapers, lists of churches, schools, organizations, and photographs were included, such as this picture of city leaders. From left to right are J. H. Fryer, post master; John Knight, pound master; Mike Messerschmidt, alderman; Lyman M. Goodhue, former mayor; Walter Parish; H. Arveson; P. Dillon; S. H. Tuttle, weed commissioner; and Oscar Smith. This photograph was taken by Harlan P. Goodman. (Library; Fran Achen Collection.)

THE RAINCOAT FACTORY. The Kinzie Rubber Company, established in 1917, was once the largest manufacturer of raincoats in the Midwest. In 1927, it became the Whitewater Garment Company. During World War II, the company employed 450 people at its Whitewater Street location, but by 1962 the number had dropped to 39, when it had the distinction of being the first company in the United States to make plastic coats. It was a Perry family operation all those years, with Leo Perry the original founder and proprietor. (Library; Fran Achen Collection.)

SNOW REMOVAL AT THE STATION. Whitewater had a section crew that cleaned the switches and road crossings. Here the semaphore stands tall with the men; it was used to signal trains coming into the station. The snow on the engines tells a story in itself. It was common in those days to run several engines between stations to keep the tracks open. (Library; Fran Achen Collection.)

ANOTHER TRAIN IN THE SNOW. An item in the *Whitewater Register*: "The train service recently has been a joke. The 'big snow' two weeks ago filled up the cuts so that any passing flurry with a drifting wind behind it fills up the narrow gorge that passing trains have made and makes conditions as bad as ever. Yes, I would prefer to be the iceman than the fellow with the railroad job these days." (WHS.)

COMPANY C GOING TO CAMP. Company C boys were ordered into active duty in the Spanish-American War in late April 1898, under the command of Capt. Leverette W. Persons. They went into training at Camp Harvey, at the Milwaukee fair grounds. By late May they had arrived at the camp in Jacksonville, Florida. Here they are heading for the train on Whitewater Street. (Library; Fran Achen Collection.)

SPANISH-AMERICAN TROOPS COMING HOME. In camp, the boys spent many hours in the hospital fighting fevers, and a few died of disease. Letters written home give a good account of the time spent there. The war ended in August, and the boys arrived back home in the middle of September, not having seen active duty, with many to see and greet them. (Library; Fran Achen Collection.)

THE OLD SORGHUM MILL. This *c.* 1900 photograph shows the mill, located on the east side of Whitewater, using (two) horse power. Farmer Abraham Hackett is standing on the right. He lived on Oak Street, in the vicinity. (Library; Fran Achen Collection.)

WILL HACKETT AND THE MILK WAGON. In July 1896, an item in the news stated Will Hackett was dipping milk for his old neighbors in place of John Dorr. In April the following year they wrote: "our milkman, Will Hackett, came out with a shining new milk wagon this morning." In the late fall, he was on the sick list, and had to send a substitute. By December 9, the news reported that he would not be seen in his milk wagon again, and that milkmen Ridge and Clemons would take the route, which they purchased a bit later. (Library; Fran Achen Collection.)

WANNA PLAY? At the Hackett Home we see a painted frame home and some family members contemplating a game of croquet in the early 1900s. Ella Hackett, the second wife of Abraham, and Marie Moyse (Gross) are pictured, along with young Sidney Hackett, who was born in 1886. (Library; Fran Achen Collection.)

WHITEWATER'S FIRST STREET SWEEPER. Harley Hackett was the son of Abraham and Mary Ridge Hackett, born in 1874. In November 1912, he was struck by lightening while getting a load of cornstalks on his farm east of town. Permanently injured, he was forced to leave his farm and move into town. He did odd jobs until 1919, when the city hired him to clean streets. He took pride in his work, and visitors would tell him they were the cleanest they had seen. On October 26, 1945, Hackett accidentally drowned while dumping his cart at the edge of the lake. (Hackett family.)

EDWIN D. COE AND THE WHITEWATER REGISTER. In 1873, Edwin D. Coe became the editor (and publisher) of the *Whitewater Register*, a local weekly founded in 1857 by H. L. and L. H. Rann. Much of what is understood today about Whitewater's past must be credited to the many passages dedicated to it in the *Whitewater Register* over the years. With this new beginning under Edwin Coe, 128 years of family leadership were to follow. Coe edited from 1873 until 1902, when his son, Robert, took over. Robert continued to ply the keys until his death in 1952. His nephews Ellsworth S. and Charles D. Coe became his partners in 1936 and continued as coeditors and copublisher after his death. After Ellsworth died, in 1958, Charles stayed on, until 1982. Then the last of the Coe publishers, Charles "Tom" Coe, took over. But the Coe era ended when, on Friday, August 17, 2001, the *Whitewater Register* was sold to Southern Lakes Newspapers, headquartered in Burlington, Wisconsin. Edwin was a true champion in publishing the facts and writing up special items related to some of the photographs in this book. They are found nowhere else, and history lies within its pages. Old copies of the *Whitewater Register* can be read on microfilm at the Irvin L. Young Memorial Library. (WHS.)

A Long Look at Whitewater.
Fran Achen came to Whitewater in 1938, a skinny, curly-haired kid with a professional box-style camera. Throughout the years he took countless photographs with it and many other cameras: portraits, wedding pictures, events for the *Whitewater Register,* or whatever caught his eye. In later years he began to print images from old, almost forgotten glass plate negatives and ended up giving Whitewater a priceless, irreplaceable gift: images of its youth. Local highlights, sporting events, aerial views of the town, and the beauty of the surrounding farmland—all these were preserved in his vast collection. Fran Achen was an admirer of Ansel Adams and Edward S. Curtis (an area native), but his main inspiration lay here in Whitewater, and he always had his camera along to capture it. (Achen family.)

A Friend in Need. A neighbor's illness brought these farmers together to plow one day in 1950, and Fran Achen was called to record it. Achen captured many such images from the surrounding countryside during his years in Whitewater (1938–2004). (Achen family.)

A Note

from the Author

Whitewater is not the busy little metropolis it was over a hundred years ago. Today, we are working to revitalize some of it, in part by gleaning those sources of yore that did their best to pass on to us what they could. It is imperative that we do not erase the scenes they put before us. We must try to educate our children that the past is fully as important as the future, so that they understand the challenges our forebearers faced in creating out city.

Many other individuals have seen the value of preserving our past, and I am indebted to them for their foresight, and for allowing me to include some of their keepsakes in this book. I urge any of you, if you have a keepsake to offer for preservation, to please share it with the Whitewater Historical Society or the Irvin L. Young Memorial Library, where most of Whitewater's records are kept.

And don't forget the columns in the local newspapers that are available on microfilm from 1855 on. These can still be browsed and enjoyed today, and offer a rich and nuanced view of our past.

I would have liked to included other scenes, and there are many other histories that remain to be written. Maybe, someday, another book or books can be put together. Several accounts are being written: the history of our police department has just been completed and one of the fire department is in the works. There is much to be talked about there, as before the fire department was formed in 1871, many city blocks were destroyed by fire.

What about our involvement in the wars? Our sports achievements? Our artists: poets, authors, artists, photographers, song writers, and others? And the famed industries that put Whitewater on the map with their superior products? And the small businesses that helped sustain the community so long ago?

Whitewater is your city, and much enjoyment can be found in piecing together the facts. First we were the "greatest," then the "Inland Banner City of the Midwest," and later, "the City Beautiful." There is a lot out there.

I hope you have enjoyed the brief view of Whitewater that has been given to you in this book, and some of the stories that I have tried to include. There are many more to be discovered and shared. If you want to share your memories with me, you can find me most mornings chatting about the old days at the McDonalds on Main Street, and another group meets regularly at Novak's. These are our modern Busy Bees.

Thank you, folks.

—Fred Kraege

Visit us at
arcadiapublishing.com